Water Rates and Related Charges

AWWA MANUAL M26

First Edition

FOUNDED 1881

American Water Works Association

American Water Works Association
6666 West Quincy Ave.
Denver, CO 80235

Printed in USA

ISBN 0-89867-362-3

Contents

Acknowledgments

The AWWA Management Division Board of Trustees gratefully acknowledges the contribution made by members of the Rates and Charges Subcommittee in preparing this manual. The committee's efforts in developing this manual contribute to meeting the need for improved methods of assigning costs to special rates and charges for water service.

Appreciation is expressed to C.E. Woods, a past chairman of the Management Division, whose personal dedication and leadership as chairman of the Rates and Charges Subcommittee made this publication a reality. Appreciation is also extended to those members of the committee who drafted the initial manuscript. They are as follows:

V.F. Pennacchio, J.D. Russell, and R.A. Smith
Chapter 1—Dedicated-Capacity Charges

J.R. Tompkins, R.S. Knight, and T.R. Stack
Chapter 2—Rates and Charges for Fire-Protection Service

G.W. Johnstone, R.F. Banker, and F.P. Griffith Jr.
Chapter 3—Capital Contributions

C.E. Woods and T.A. Scott
Chapter 4—Ancillary Charges

All members of the committee reviewed the manuscript and made constructive recommendations for revision. Issues involving final changes in organization and content were mutually resolved by an editorial committee.

The management division is sincerely indebted to the entire committee for their time, expertise, and exchange of views which is evident in the context of this manual.

*   *   *

Rates and Charges Subcommittee

C.E. Woods (Chairman),* Consultant, South Central Connecticut Regional Water Authority, Palm Harbor, Fla.

G.W. Johnstone (Vice Chairman),* American Water Works Service Company, Haddon Heights, N.J.

R.F. Banker (Past Chairman),* Black & Veatch, Kansas City, Mo.

F.P. Griffith Jr., Fairfax County Water Authority, Merrifield, Va.

*Member of Rates and Charges Editorial Committee.

C.R. Harrison, Clackamas Water District, Clackamas, Ore.
R.S. Knight, St. Louis County Water Company, St. Louis, Mo.
M.D. Ludlum, Seattle Water Department, Seattle, Wash.
Fred Moriarty, Peat, Marwick, Mitchell & Co., St. Louis, Mo.
V.F. Pennacchio, Coffin & Richardson, Inc., Boston, Mass.
J.D. Russell, John D. Russell Associates, Inc., Milwaukee, Wis.
T.A. Scott, Denver Water Department, Denver, Colo.
R.A. Smith, General Motors Corporation, Detroit, Mich.
T.R. Stack, Illinois Commerce Commission, Springfield, Ill.
W.M. Stout, Gannett Fleming Water Resources Engineers, Inc., Harrisburg, Pa.
J.R. Tompkins, Middlesex Water Company, Iselin, N.J.

AWWA Management Division Liaison Representative

R.L. Wubbena, Economic & Engineering Services, Inc., Olympia, Wash.

Introduction

The American Water Works Association (AWWA) strongly advocates that a properly operated and managed water utility should be a self-sufficient enterprise. Through the AWWA Management Division and its working committees, AWWA has developed a series of manuals and programs that provide guidance for achieving self-sufficiency in utility operations.

In 1983, AWWA Manual M1, *Water Rates*, was updated to include recommended approaches for the development of cost-based general water-service rates. The manual describes two methods for preparing cost-allocation studies and presents a variety of generally accepted forms for general water-rate structures. The manual also recognizes that general water rates alone may not be sufficient to establish an equitable and fully cost-based system of charges.

In establishing a system of rates and related charges, the utility should consider its growth rate, capital construction programs, and financing requirements, as well as certain services that may be performed for only a limited number of the utility's customers. Thus, a broader system of rates and charges may be necessary to achieve a fully "cost-based," self-sufficient enterprise.

As an example, when addressing the question of system expansion to serve new-customer growth, the use of a single system of general water rates may impose inappropriate costs on existing customers. The same problem may occur with various one-time ancillary services necessary for only a limited number of the utility's customers. In order to distribute those costs that are not common to all customers and also achieve administrative efficiency, a separate schedule of utility prices or charges may be required.

This manual was developed to complement AWWA Manual M1. It examines some of the issues associated with the design of a total system of water rates and related charges and addresses periodic or regularly assigned charges and procedures that are associated with one-time charges.

Chapter 1 discusses two types of dedicated-capacity charges generally defined in this manual as availability and demand contract charges. These charges may be appropriate for use by an expanding utility or for large customers, and they can play an important part in allocating the cost of service to benefiting customers.

Chapter 2 expands on the discussion presented in AWWA Manual M1 of costs and charges related to providing fire-protection service to a municipality, fire district, property owner, or customer who benefits from the service provided.

Chapters 3 and 4 examine some of the issues and procedures associated with one-time charges used by a water utility. Chapter 3 looks at several approaches to calculating a system-development charge or up-front equity payment. The chapter discusses the system buy-in and the incremental-cost pricing methods used to calculate a system-development charge. Chapter 4 discusses common types of ancillary charges used by the industry to reduce the administrative and customer-support costs assigned to general water rates. These charges should generally be assigned only to those customers who benefit from the service and who are responsible for the costs being incurred.

This manual includes a glossary of terms commonly used in the rate-setting process by water utilities. This glossary is an important step in establishing uniformity of the terms used to define costs and methods of allocating costs for providing water utility service. The glossary will be expanded as additional AWWA rate and accounting manuals are developed.

The AWWA water-rate manuals should be used as guides for the recommended procedures and practices used in developing cost-of-service analyses and establishing a system of rates and charges that meet the objective of being cost-based, fair, and reasonable. It is recognized that local conditions, policies, and regulatory and/or contract constraints may limit the full implementation of some methods for allocating costs and designing rates and charges. As conditions change, these manuals can provide guidance for the conversion to a full system of cost-based rates and related charges.

Chapter 1

Dedicated-Capacity Charges

For some water utilities, it may be appropriate to include some form of dedicated-capacity charge as part of their total rates and charges program. This type of charge is instituted to ensure that the utility will recover, from those for whom a significant portion of the total utility-plant facilities capacity has been dedicated, the ongoing costs associated with this capacity. Two types of dedicated-capacity charges are the availability charge and the demand contract charge.

AVAILABILITY CHARGE

In this manual, the term *availability charge* describes a charge made to recover capital-related costs and other ongoing costs incurred by a utility when it is constructing facilities for the benefit of potential future customers. When used, the charge is normally part of the utility's general water-rate structure. It is made only between the time service is first made available to a potential customer and the time service actually goes into effect. Thereafter, the normal water-rate structure takes over and the availability charge is terminated.

The justification for an availability charge is that the utility incurs a number of costs regardless of whether or not direct service is being rendered. Under certain circumstances, it may be reasonable to charge for simply having service available to a potential customer's property although, for some reason, the service is not being used.

The major need for an availability charge is in new water systems in which the immediate connected-customer base is small but where a certain minimum level of revenue is necessary to make the installation of a water system financially feasible. There may be other situations where use of an availability charge is appropriate. However, in each case, the principal need and basis for the charges would be because a utility has made a substantial investment in plant facilities and incurred costs to make water service available. Under these conditions, it is appropriate for such costs to be shared by both connected users and potential future users of the water facilities.

Even in those situations where the utility has an effective program for customer contribution of capital covering mains and other local facilities, the utility can incur fixed costs and other costs for backup facilities. These costs should be shared between existing customers and those noncustomer property owners who may derive benefits from the facilities. An example would be an investment in water utility facilities that are built to meet the demand of a large, new land development. Often a developer will lay out all of the lots, and the utility will build facilities to meet the water-supply needs for the total area to be developed. Thus, the plant has been designed and built with the capacity to meet the needs of all potential customers. Costs initially incurred will be substantially higher than would be required for the initial connected-customer base. This happens even when all of the mains or other local facilities have been paid for by the developer. The ongoing costs of the reserve capacity can be recovered through an availability charge. In this way, all property owners who benefit continuously pay their share of the costs. Although an availability charge has had only limited use in the industry, it can be an effective element in a rate schedule.

Another application of the availability charge would be in a situation where a utility folds most of the cost of public fire service into its general water-service rates. Property owners near to, but not connected to, the mains may also benefit from the availability of public fire service; however, these property owners technically are not customers. An availability charge could be used so that they pay their share of the benefit received from public fire-protection service.

There are statutes in some states concerning the use of availability charges, and it is advisable to become familiar with these statutes as well as any legal precedents or laws that could affect the use of these charges. Regulated utilities should also research the policies and requirements of their regulatory agency in the use of availability charges.

In establishing the form of and amount of an availability charge, the first step is to determine the facilities for which related costs are to be included in the charge. Costs should include certain capital-related expenses and operating and maintenance expenses. Table 1-1 illustrates the procedure for calculating an availability charge.

The final step in the development of an availability charge is to establish the unit basis for the charge. Table 1-1 lists an equivalent-customer basis. Bases other than the equivalent-customer basis could be used for establishing unit charges.

The actual annual cost for a particular utility would be used in developing its cost data and resulting charge. For investor-owned utilities, depreciation expense, return on rate base, and all applicable taxes would be part of the cost to be recovered.

DEMAND CONTRACT CHARGE

The fixed costs for the base- and the extra-capacity requirements of a water system are allocated to the various cost components, and general water-use rates are designed to recover these costs. This concept is described in AWWA Manual M1, under the section "Distribution of Costs to Customer Classes: Base—Extra Capacity Method." As a general

Table 1-1 Example Calculation of Availability Charge

Total investment by the utility in plant facilities to be included in availability charge	$450 000
Annual costs	
Debt service	45 000
Payment in lieu of taxes	30 000
Projected annual cost for inspection, billing, and certain operation and maintenance expenses	45 000
	$120 000
Monthly charge based on 2000 equivalent potential customers	$5.00

*Based on government-owned utility.

rule, this procedure works well for classes of customers that have many diversified customer units. Single-family residential customers would be an example of such a class. Loss of one or a few customers from this class would have little impact on the financial condition of the utility because the reduced use and revenue would not be great in relationship to the total revenue to be derived from the utility system. The same principle would apply when fixed costs are allocated using the commodity–demand method, also discussed in AWWA Manual M1.

When there is only one or, at most, a few large customers whose use and revenue is significant to the system, loss of a customer could adversely impact the water utility's financial condition. In these situations, the utility may want to consider alternative rate procedures to recover the fixed costs associated with serving these customers. One such procedure would be the use of a dedicated-capacity charge incorporated into a contract whereby the water customer agrees to pay the fixed costs associated with a specific share of the utility's capacity and related investment. In this manual, such an arrangement is termed a *demand contract.*

A demand contract would be used when a large customer needs a firm supply of water that would be a significant portion of the total capacity of the utility. In some instances, the utility may be dedicating existing capacity or it may be required to add capacity to meet this need. Under these conditions, it is to the benefit of both the utility and the customer to establish a service contract that sets forth the terms under which water utility service will be provided. Customers contracting for a given capacity should agree to pay the fixed costs related to that capacity for a stated period of time. The term *take or pay contract* has been used to describe a demand contract because the customer pays whether or not the water is taken.

The contract requires the utility to commit itself to the long-term capital and operating costs of a significant portion of its facilities and provides assurance that the fixed costs related to that capacity will be paid by the intended customer. Without such an agreement, other customers would have to pick up the fixed costs related to the lost water sales if the large customer were to shut down operations or otherwise not use the capacity built for it.

Elements of charges under demand contracts may include, but are not necessarily limited to, an annual charge for the agreed rate of flow that may be exerted on the system, which will cover the fixed costs related to that demand, and a charge per unit of volume to cover the commodity costs (typically chemicals, power, and other volume-related costs) of the actual water use during the billing period, together with any related overhead or administrative expenses.

Such a contract will typically contain provisions that govern the following kinds of conditions under which service will be provided:

- starting date and length of the agreement;
- types of service—water use, fire protection;
- service standards—water quality, pressure;
- conditions of service, including any limitations for annual, seasonal, peak day, and hourly rates of use;
- provisions, procedures, and planning requirements to effect changes in use;
- rates and charges for service;
- provisions and procedures for changing rates;
- payment procedures—billing date, payment date, rate payment penalties, etc.;
- provisions for planned or unplanned interruption of service by supplier;
- special requirements and costs for special equipment, backup facilities, provisions for any customer advance of capital, etc.;
- meter-test and reading-verification procedures and adjustments for faulty metering;
- means for resolution of disputes;
- renewal provisions; and
- conditions for termination of contract.

A contract for certain dedicated capacity should also have appropriate provisions to ensure that the financial commitments can be met. A contract for payment for a given demand not only protects the other customers of the system, but may be quite essential in financing any needed system expansion. As an example, when a government-owned utility issues revenue bonds to finance system expansion, the bond-rating agencies and the investors they represent require reasonable assurance as to the security of the revenue projections supporting the investment. Such security is enhanced greatly by a demand contract between the utility and a customer in sound financial condition.

One form of potential security for backing a demand contract is a surety bond that is issued by a reliable bonding agency and that guarantees the payment of contract obligations incurred by the customer, if necessary. Careful investigation of the costs and enforceability of such a bond is essential. Also, for regulated utilities, approval by the regulator may be necessary.

The concepts described in this chapter can be modified and adapted to meet the specific needs of individual water utilities. There are a number of variations in the use of these charges not covered in this general discussion of dedicated-capacity charges. By a careful analysis of the relevant operating and cost characteristics of each water utility, a system of dedicated-capacity charges can be designed to meet specific needs while adhering to the concept of sound cost-related water rates.

Chapter 2

Rates and Charges for Fire-Protection Service

AWWA Manual M1 gives an example of how fire-protection and general water-service costs are calculated through an overall cost-of-service study. The example illustrates the various cost-allocation principles involved in such a study. In a full cost-based system of water rates, the total cost allocated to fire service is the amount of revenues that the water utility should receive for its provision of this service. A properly designed cost-of-service study requires that the cost of providing fire service be calculated. Once the total cost is established, the utility must then devise the appropriate methods to further allocate this cost and derive revenues from those served.

In the example cited, all costs are charged to public fire protection, and a unit-price basis of charge is calculated using the total number of public fire hydrants in the water system. Multiplying the unit price by the number of hydrants allows the costs to be assigned to the municipalities served. In turn, the municipalities pass on these costs to individual taxpayers, possibly as part of the ad valorem or other taxes assessed on property owners. Assuming a close relationship between the relative amount of taxes paid by an individual taxpayer (or class of taxpayers) and the fire protection required for the property, the fair portion of the total cost of public fire service will be borne by each taxpayer.

This chapter will examine the issues associated with fire-protection service that were beyond the scope of AWWA Manual M1. This chapter does, in effect, expand the work of AWWA Manual M1 by describing alternative methods that may be used to charge individual customers of a utility or the property owners in municipalities for their fair share of the total fire-protection revenue requirement.

HISTORICAL PERSPECTIVE

The concepts, policies, procedures, and practices related to fire-protection-service charges have evolved over the past 100 years. During this period, numerous papers setting forth differing theories and opinions concerning the establishment of rates and charges have been published and debated. In 1888, F.L. Fuller authored the first paper published by AWWA on the subject of fire-service rates and charges. This was followed, in 1911, by a study by Metcalf, Kuichling, and Hawley. The authors proposed a method to prorate costs between general water service and fire service based on the comparison of the capacity of the facilities required. A joint report, published in 1951 by the committees of the American Society of Civil Engineers and the Section of Municipal Law of the American Bar Association, reviewed some of the problems of cost allocation for joint facilities used to provide both general water and fire-protection services. In 1954, an AWWA committee produced a report, "Determination of Water Rate Schedules," a part of which was related to fire-protection charges. In 1955, *Water and Sewerage Works* published an article by Darrell A. Root and Thomas R. Camp, titled "Equitable Charges for Fire Protection." In 1971, the AWWA Committee on Financial Aspects of Fire Prevention and Protection presented a report on the subject. The committee report subsequently was published in the 1974 *Journal AWWA*.

A review of these publications documents three general methods for the allocation of costs between general water service and fire-protection service. The methods are:

- allocation of primary cost to general water service with incremental cost allocated to fire-protection service,
- allocation of primary cost to fire-protection service with incremental cost allocated to general water service, and
- allocation of cost to both general water service and fire-protection service on a proportional basis.

It is important to note that each of these three methods will result in significantly different costs allocated to fire-protection service. The current community and utility needs should determine which of the three cost-allocation methods is most appropriate.

THE PROCESS

The process of developing a rate structure for assessing the costs of fire-protection service to customers consists of the following steps:

1. Establish the method of cost allocation to be used.
2. Calculate the total cost of providing fire-protection service (refer to the analysis in AWWA Manual M1 for the proportional-cost method), which forms the basis for the portion of the utility's total revenue requirement to be provided by fire-protection-service charges. Where applicable, these total costs are further allocated between public and private fire-protection services.
3. Establish a policy that specifies the billing units to use, such as number of hydrants, inch-feet of mains, or number of individual customers or classes of customer.
4. Determine number of hydrants, units of inch-feet of mains, or number of customers to be used as a basis for determining unit costs.
5. Calculate rates.
6. Apply rates to unit quantities to ensure that the rates will produce desired levels of revenues.

Allocation Method

One important consideration in establishing which method of cost allocation to use is the particular requirements of the communities being served by the water utility. If it is determined that both fire service and general water service must be given equal weight in design and development of the water system, then the proportional-cost method should be used. If it is determined that general water service is the principal purpose of the water utility system with fire service being important yet supplemental, then the method requiring that primary cost be allocated to general service and incremental cost be allocated to fire service may be adopted. In situations where fire protection is of principal importance, then the method requiring allocation of primary cost to fire protection and incremental cost to general water service may be appropriate. Such a situation might occur in industrial areas where fire service, not general water service, is the primary consideration.

The proportional-cost method was used for the example given in AWWA Manual M1. However, it was emphasized that the requirements of the individual utility must be considered when selecting the appropriate allocation method. The decision regarding the appropriate method must be based on an analysis of the factors affecting the community and the demands to be placed on the water system. After having made that decision, the cost of fire service to the utility is established and a method is developed for charging the customers.

Cost Calculation

The allocated investment in backup utility-plant facilities together with the net investment in hydrants, hydrant laterals, fire-service meters, fire-service lines, and other plant facilities used solely for fire-protection service are used to determine total investment for fire service. This becomes the basis for calculating the proper share of the annual capital-related costs of the utility that are applicable to fire-protection service. Operation and maintenance expenses are allocated in a manner similar to investment.

AWWA Manual M1 gives a more detailed explanation and illustration of the allocation process. The remainder of this chapter presents points be considered when allocating total fire-protection costs between private fire protection and public fire protection and when developing charges to meet the allocated costs.

PRIVATE FIRE-PROTECTION CHARGES

The costs of providing private fire-protection service to individual properties represent a service not directly benefiting the general customer population of the utility. Such a service provides a measurable benefit that can reasonably be charged for through a system of rates and charges to those customers receiving private fire-protection service.

The advantages of installing private fire-service systems, including hydrants, automatic sprinkler systems, and standpipes, are obvious. Automatic sprinkler systems and standpipes are essential in large buildings and benefit the property owner by improving control over fire, decreasing injury to personnel, decreasing property damage, and markedly reducing annual insurance costs.

The costs of providing private fire-protection service should be charged to the property owner. The pricing techniques relate to how the cost should be determined and how it should be billed to the individual property owner. Under a system of rates that are cost based, these charges should be determined on the basis of the actual cost of rendering the service and not on the value of the fire protection to the user.

When a utility provides private fire service to customers placing fire-protection demands on the system, the related costs should not be recovered through the public fire-service charge, but rather these costs should be borne directly by the private fire-service customers.

The private fire-service rate should include capital-related costs for the utility's investment in on-site private fire-service facilities, such as the fire-service line, detector check and meter, meter and valve pit, and any special check valves or other valves that are part of the utility facilities. In addition to the capital-servicing costs related to the on-site facilities are the annual operation and maintenance costs and other costs of these facilities.

It is essential to determine the portion of total fire-protection-service costs related to backup facilities that is allocatable to private fire protection. The allocation of costs to total fire service was previously described; one method for the subdivision of those costs to private and public categories is by the use of a demand basis whereby a 6-in. private fire-service-line demand is equated to a 6-in. hydrant-lateral demand. Some other basis of weighting may be used when appropriate.

The private fire-protection charge can take the form of a fixed annual fee or other periodic fee. This will vary with the size of the fire-service connection because there is a substantial difference in the potential demand of differing sizes of private fire-service connections. Although basing charges on a size of connection is a simple way in which private fire-protection rates can be designed, some utilities prefer to charge according to the number of private fire hydrants, automatic sprinkler systems, and standpipes on each service. The administration of this form of charge is difficult; therefore, the administrative time, cost, and relative benefits associated with policing the private fire-service systems of the customer should be considered.

PUBLIC FIRE-PROTECTION CHARGES

The form of public fire-protection-service charges is often based on long-standing precedent within the utility. It is usually the result of operating conditions and policy considerations at the time that the first set of fire-service rates was established.

Service is often provided to more than one agency responsible for public fire service. A series of rates may be developed to allocate the cost to individual communities or fire districts in an equitable way. Methods of charging, either through the tax system or through utility water rates, may then be devised so that individual customers or property owners can be assessed their respective shares of this total cost. The most common forms of rates in use are

- a hydrant charge for each public fire hydrant,
- an inch-foot charge based on the number of inch-feet of transmission and distribution mains serving each agency,
- a combination hydrant charge and inch-foot charge based on the number of inch-feet of transmission and distribution mains serving each municipality,
- a lump-sum annual charge to each agency responsible for public fire service, and
- a direct service charge to individual customers in situations where a utility cannot, for policy, legal, regulatory, or legislative reasons, charge the agency served for public fire service.

Some people believe that since public fire protection is a public-service function it should be charged for through the tax system on the property in the municipality being provided the service. This would mean that the total cost and resulting revenue requirement for public fire service should be charged to the municipality and then collected from individual property owners through the ad valorem or some other tax system. The availability of public fire protection reduces insurance premiums; consequently, there is a relationship between benefit and payment for fire service. This relationship is based on the value of the property, and by assigning costs to the municipal entities, revenues derived will also vary with the value protected. As an example, a single-family home of wooden construction may have an assessed value of $50 000. Because of the type of construction, this house would potentially require a higher fire demand than a single-family home of masonry construction with an assessed value of $150 000. Yet, under an ad valorem tax system, the owners of the masonry constructed house would pay three times as much for public fire-protection service than would the owners of the wood house.

In those instances where the utility adds the cost of fire service to the general water-service charge, some noncustomers could benefit from public fire protection without paying for their share. An example would be property owners who are situated near a public fire hydrant but who are not connected to mains of the utility. These individuals would have private sources of water, such as wells. A fire-service-availability charge, as discussed in Chapter 1, can sometimes correct this inequity.

When using the property tax system to collect fire-protection costs, property exempt from the ad valorem tax system would not pay for any public fire-protection service. Where a

Table 2-1 Public and Private Fire-Protection Service Charges Using Equivalent-Connection Method

		Total	Public	Private
Costs to be prorated		$110 900	$ 85 400	$25 500
Direct costs—hydrants		57 000	57 000	—
Direct costs—private firelines		9 200	—	9 200
		$177 100	$142 400	$34 700
	Number	Size Factor	Equivalent 6-in. Connections	Allocation
Town A hydrants	388	1.0	388	
Town B hydrants	255	1.0	255	
Town C hydrants	512	1.0	512	
	1155		1155	77%
Private fire services				
4-in. service lines	100	0.44	44	
6-in. service lines	200	1.00	200	
8-in. service lines	60	1.72	103	
	360		347	23%
Total equivalent 6-in. connections			1502	100%
Public charge per connection				
Cost per hydrant	$123.30 per year			
Private charge per connection				
4-in. service	$ 44 per year			
6-in. service	100 per year			
8-in. service	172 per year			

large percentage of the property is so classified, the use of an add-on to the utility's service-charge rate might result in a fairer recovery of costs.

Table 2-1 shows an example allocation of total fire-protection costs between public and private categories and the method of deriving rates for public and private fire service using the equivalent fire-connection method. As reflected in this example, the public charge per hydrant connection is derived by dividing the total annual public cost of $142 400 by the 1155 equivalent connections, resulting in a $123.30 annual charge for each 6-in. hydrant connection.

The private fire-protection charges are derived by dividing the annual private cost of $34 700 by the 347 equivalent connections, resulting in a $100 charge for each 6-in. connection. The charge for other sizes recognizes their differing capacities.

It should be recognized that the charge per public hydrant connection is simply a method of expressing total annual public fire-protection-related costs on the basis of some measurable unit. It is only incidentally related to the actual number of hydrants. Agencies reviewing proposed fire-service charges sometimes fail to realize that a charge per fire hydrant is not limited to the costs of the hydrant alone, but is due to the total costs allocated to public fire service.

A second method used to develop charges for public fire service is through a combination of hydrant/inch-foot elements. The hydrant charge is first developed to cover the fixed costs associated with the investment and maintenance of hydrants. The remaining costs generally relate to the demand requirements of the fire-protection service and can be assigned to each jurisdiction on the basis of inch-feet of transmission and distribution mains located therein. In addition, large-diameter transmission mains that serve several jurisdictions may be distributed on the basis of population or other appropriate criteria in order to

Table 2-2 Public Fire-Protection Service Charges Using Hydrant/Inch-Foot Method

Public fire-service cost from Table 2-1

Hydrants	$ 57 000
Demand	85 400
	$142 400

Town	Inch-Feet	Hydrants
A	3 982 000	388
B	2 613 000	255
C	10 485 000	512
	17 080 000	1155

Inch-foot rate

$85 400/17 080 000 = $0.0050/inch-foot

Hydrant charge

$$\frac{\$57\,000}{1155} = \$49.35/\text{hydrant}$$

Annual Charges

	Inch-Foot			Hydrant			
Town	No.	Rate	Amount	No.	Rate	Amount	Total
A	3 982 000	$0.0050	$19 910	388	$49.35	$19 148	$ 39 058
B	2 613 000	0.0050	13 065	255	49.35	12 585	25 650
C	10 485 000	0.0050	52 425	512	49.35	25 267	77 692
Total	17 080 000		$85 400	1155		$57 000	$142 400

Table 2-3 Public Fire-Protection Charges to Individual Utility Customers Using Relative Fire-Flow Requirements Method

Town	Class of Customer	Customers	Fire Flow Used*	Equivalent Customers	Revenues
A	Residential	5 700	1.0	5 700	$ 43 434
B	Residential	3 700	1.0	3 700	28 194
C	Residential	6 620	1.0	6 620	50 444
	Commercial	1 080	2.25	2 430	18 511
	Industrial	60	4.0	240	1 829
		17 160		18 690	$142 412

Annual rate per equivalent customer

$142 400/18 690 = $7.62

Rates — Residential 1.0 × $7.62 = $ 7.62
Commercial 2.25 × $7.62 = 17.14
Industrial 4.0 × $7.62 = 30.48

*Represents relative demand placed on the system by all customer classes with residential customers constituting the base.

give recognition to varying demand requirements. Table 2-2 shows an example of the apportionment of public fire-service costs among three towns on a hydrant/inch-foot basis and the development of an inch-foot charge.

In those jurisdictions where for policy, regulatory, legal, or legislative reasons a fire-service charge cannot be made to a town or fire district, the total revenues can simply be derived directly from the utility's customers. The alternative approach would be to assign to classes of customers a cost based on the relative fire-service demand for each class. If this is done, the amount so allocated can be added to the individual customer service charge developed for general water service or may be added to the customer's bill as a separate fire-service fee. Table 2-3 illustrates an example of the apportionment of public fire-service costs among various classes of customers, recognizing their relative fire-service demands and the development of average annual charges for each customer in the class.

Regardless of the method used for setting fire-protection-service rates, it should be based on a total revenue requirement equal to the allocated cost of providing this service. Policies and practices in the adoption of rates and charges for fire-protection service have evolved to meet the needs of individual utilities and the communities they serve. Legislative, legal, policy, and regulatory constraints, as well as past practice, must be considered in rate planning for future utility revenue needs from fire-protection service. When such rates are based on the foundation of a sound cost-allocation procedure, which provides a close relationship between the cost of service and the revenue to be derived from the customer, the utility is in a strong position to receive public acceptance of its rates.

Chapter 3

Capital Contributions

Water-supply problems throughout the nation are created by a wide range of hydrologic, topographic, water-source, and urban conditions. To cope with these varied conditions, individual water utilities may require one or more of the following system improvements:

- expanding the quantity of water supply available for normal weather periods, droughts, and emergencies for existing customers;
- source-of-supply protection from potential or actual contaminants, and treatment facilities necessary to assure water-quality compliance with new or upgraded standards;
- additional distribution, storage, or pumping capacity to meet system-expansion needs for both fire service and general water service;
- upgrading and replacement of older facilities to improve reliability, reduce maintenance and repair costs, increase capacity, and meet today's standards; and
- expansion of the system to provide service to new customers and developing areas.

Most water utilities must make capital construction expenditures for system improvements. The utility must develop the revenue and establish financing programs needed to meet the projected costs of these improvements. A utility should determine which costs are best met by adjustments of the general water rates and which costs may best be met by some form of capital contribution.

Construction expenditures result in a need to raise and service large amounts of capital. Each water utility has its own unique institutional, operational, financial, and regulatory considerations, and the utility must evaluate the financing options that best meet its capital requirements.

Replacement of or addition to existing facilities that were purchased in the past at relatively low costs and interest rates requires significant increases in both capital and interest costs. For example, a main installed many years ago at \$4.00/ft with 5-percent interest financing may cost \$20.00/ft with 10-percent interest when replaced today. Many utilities faced with rapid development within their service areas find that the current costs of extending service to these areas will also place a large burden on their existing customers.

Given this situation, a conflict arises between fairness and resource-allocation considerations. Economic theory suggests that all customers should pay the same water rates and that pricing should use the incremental cost. This may produce excess revenues over current cost requirements. Efficiency in resource-allocation considerations must be balanced against concerns for fairness. It can be argued that existing customers should not have to pay higher water rates attributable to the higher costs caused by requirements of new customers.

FRONT-END CAPITAL PAYMENT

When new investment to serve growth does not financially or indirectly benefit existing customers (reduce operating costs, restore or enhance system reliability, etc.), it could be considered unfair to apply rate increases to these customers as a result of this growth. One financing method that may be considered in handling system growth is a front-end capital payment (customer contribution), either in conjunction with or in the absence of local utility bond financing or other capital means. A front-end capital payment can be used to create fairness and some degree of efficiency in resource allocation.

Any method or combination of methods used to develop front-end capital payments should be tailored to the needs of the individual utility. Available data about the system's operating characteristics, the rate of new-customer growth, capital requirements, and available financing programs will influence the methodology used to develop the front-end capital payment. The justification for front-end customer contributions of capital is based on fairness to existing customers for financing utility-plant facilities required because of new-customer growth. In some situations, institutional constraints may preclude full use of such procedures. Potential short- and/or long-term economic impacts on the community might require extension of the existing system to foster other local governmental policies.

The policies of regulatory agencies governing investor-owned utilities must be taken into account when developing capital-financing programs for new customers. The effect on existing capital obligations must also be considered where covenants and other debt or equity provisions may restrict the use of certain types of financing. Also, for investor-owned systems, the Internal Revenue Service (IRS) must be considered. The IRS has ruled that some contributions by the customer constitute taxable income. The use of customer-contributed capital for mains and other plant facilities has affected the amount of depreciation expense or investment tax credit to which the utility is entitled. For these and other reasons, investor-owned utilities must take all of these factors into account to avoid any adverse consequences that might impact customer rates.

The growth of customer-service areas for many water utilities ordinarily takes place in the form of subdivision development. Increasingly, developers are being required to install and pay for all or a substantial portion of local on-site facilities. In many instances, the developer and, ultimately, the property owner are required to pay for the costs of service lines, meters, hydrants, and special pumping and storage facilities that are for the exclusive use of the development. The rules, regulations, and rates governing the extension of water mains, given in Appendix A, illustrate this type of service-extension policy.

System-Development Charges

For water utility systems experiencing substantial growth, the need to increase capacity is becoming an acute problem. With growth in the customer base, system capacity often requires expansion both to replace used up reserves and to accommodate present and future growth requirements. Utilities with substantial growth characteristics may look to new customers to pay both the cost of local facilities and some form of system-development charge as part of the capital-contribution process.

Payments such as these have been called different names in the industry, but essentially they are contributions of capital towards the development of water-system facilities required because of new-customer growth. The terms *facility charge*, *plant investment fee*, *impact fee*, and *system-development charge* all refer to a program of contributions of capital from developers or new customers connecting to a water system. In some instances, these charges cover both local facility construction costs and the construction cost for the required backup utility-plant facilities. In the context of this manual, the term *system-development charge* (SDC) is used and is limited to the contribution of capital made for the required backup plant facilities. When using this type of charge, utilities should carefully define what it includes and the circumstances under which it will be applied.

The purpose in designing customer-contributed-capital system charges is to prevent or reduce the inequity to existing customers that results when these customers must pay the increases in water rates that are needed to pay for added plant costs for new customers. Contributed capital reduces the need for new outside sources of capital, which ordinarily have been serviced from the revenue stream. Under a system of contributed capital, many water utilities are able to finance required facilities by use of a "growth pays for growth" policy. The amount of the front-end contribution will vary with the method used to determine the share of plant investment required for new customers. A common denominator and primary purpose for requiring front-end capital contributions is to permit the use of a single rate schedule applicable to both existing and new customers rather than to have cost differentiation through vintage rates. The front-end contribution may be used to finance new construction required for new customers or can result in the early retirement of bonded debt, the proceeds of which financed SDC-related facilities.

The following sections describe two methods for designing SDCs to accomplish contribution of capital to the utility. The principles discussed apply whether or not all facilities required to serve new customers, both local and/or backup plant facilities, are being considered. These techniques have been used primarily by government-owned utilities but may be equally applicable to investor-owned systems.

System buy-in method. One method of determining the amount of contribution required from new customers (or developers who represent new customers) is based on the "buy-in" concept. This concept is based on the premise that new customers are entitled to water service at the same prices charged to existing customers. However, it is also recognized that existing customers have provided funds for debt retirement, cash financing of improvements and additions to the water system through payment of water rates, or through their own contribution of capital. New customers connecting to the system should be required to pay an amount equal to that which has already been paid by existing customers towards the invested capital funds. This system buy-in method is one way in which customers can be required to pay an amount equal to the net investment in the existing plant facilities.

Several methods are used to calculate the system buy-in charge. In Table 3-1, a sample calculation is illustrated. In this example, the new customers would be required to pay for all of the costs of local facilities, such as mains, hydrants, services, and meters for the property being served. Since the new customer would be paying directly for such facilities, it would not be fair to require payment for the investments in similar facilities used to serve existing customers. Therefore, from the net investment (cost less depreciation reserve) in all utility-plant facilities, the investment in local facilities would be excluded. Since the new customer, through the rates paid, would be covering the capital carrying costs, the bond debt also would be excluded from the base. The resulting balance of net equity investment would be divided by the total number of existing customers or customer equivalents to determine the amount of payment required from the new customer to buy into the utility at a parity with existing customers.

After new customers have paid their front-end capital contribution toward backup plant facilities, they become equivalent to existing customers and share the responsibility for

Table 3-1 Illustrative Determination of System-Development Charge—System Buy-in Pricing Basis*

	Original Cost	Accumulated Depreciation	Net Cost
	($000)	($000)	($000)
Source of supply	5 000	1000	4 000
Treatment and pumping	8 000	1200	6 800
Distribution system	12 800	1800	11 000
Services, meters, and hydrants	4 800	800	4 000
General structures	1 400	200	1 200
	$32 000	$5000	$27 000
Less net cost of			
Distribution system			11 000
Services, meters, and hydrants			4 000
Net investment in backup plant			12 000
Less:			
Outstanding bonds			8 000
Total equity investment			$ 4 000
Number of customers			20 000
Average net equity investment per equivalent ⅝-in. customer			$ 200
Required SDC			$ 200

*Assumes new customers pay for all on-site facilities: mains, services, meters, and hydrants.

existing assets and liabilities, including the retirement of bonded indebtedness. When additional costs are incurred for system improvements, replacement, or expansion, all customers share in the costs of such improvements.

Because customer-use characteristics vary, it is necessary to develop a system of customer equivalents for the calculation of the buy-in amount. Customer equivalents could be expressed in terms of ⅝-in. meters. Investment in portions of the system may be related principally to the total volume of annual water use. Investment in other portions of the system may be related to maximum-day requirement or to maximum-hour needs. Thus, equivalent-customer allocations could reflect all of the important system-demand and cost characteristics in the calculation process.

Incremental-cost pricing method. When new customers connect to the water system, they will either use reserve capacity, which must then be replaced, or new capacity, which is added to meet their needs. Under the buy-in method, the new customer would pay for this use through a fee related to the embedded average-equity investment in such capacity. Under the incremental-cost pricing method, new customers would be responsible for their share of the cost of the last increment of defined system-development charge facilities and/or the increment of planned future additions to meet their needs. Also, system-development charges are designed so that new customers pay the incremental cost of system expansion as determined by either recent construction experience and/or projected costs of planned future improvements to the extent that such costs are not met from general water-service rates. Using the buy-in method, a new customer is considered to be on a parity with the existing customer based on the average-equity portion of the investment in plant facilities. The goal of the incremental-cost pricing method is to eliminate or minimize the portion of future rate increases due to growth by reducing the utility's new investment to a point at which revenue from new customers under existing rates can support the actual new investment that the utility makes for new customers.

Table 3-2 Illustrative Determination of System-Development Charge—Incremental-Cost Pricing Basis

Annual revenue under existing rates for typical ⅝-in. customer		$ 205
Less: Annual operation and maintenance expenses to be met from rates	$115	
Annual replacements and improvement costs to be met from rates	30	145
Net revenue available to service new debt		$ 60
Debt that can be serviced (assume 20-year debt amortization at 10% annual interest rate) $60 ÷ 0.1175 =		$ 510
Estimated total investment in backup facilities required to serve a new ⅝-in. customer		$1300
Net system-development charge		$ 790

*Assumes new customers pay for all on-site facilities: mains, services, meters, and hydrants.

A simplified illustration of the determination of a system-development charge using the incremental-cost pricing method is illustrated in Table 3-2. From the table it can be seen that of the total $1300 investment required to serve a new customer, the expected annual revenue under existing rates will support $510, with the remaining $790 being contributed as a system-development charge. Unless this amount of system-development charge is received from the new customer, new debt to finance the facilities needed for the customer's service could cause overall revenue requirements per customer to increase, resulting in rate increases for all customers.

The cost of plant facilities attributable to new-customer growth must be determined by evaluating either recently built new capacity or planned future capacity. Another factor to be considered is the time at which new customers are added relative to when the capital needed to support this growth is to be expended. Capital-improvement construction normally does not increase system capacity in direct proportion to customer growth. Long-range planning, economy of scale in plant sizing, and other factors must be considered in the timing of capital improvements. Facilities designed to accommodate customers for several years in the future may be financed and constructed in an early year in the cycle. This may result in the need to pay the fixed charges for the plant facilities before the capacity is used. Existing customers may be required to make these payments until such time as new customers connect, pay a system-development charge, and assume some of the burden of current payments through the general water rates for water use. Once these system-development charges are received, they can be used to pay off the sources of external capital, which will, in turn, reduce the ongoing fixed charges.

Similarly, some facilities required for new customers may not be constructed until some years after new customers have made their contribution. Thus, recognition of the time value of money, both for capital-investment expenditures and customer contributions, may be required through the application of the present-worth principle. This permits a balanced valuation of the difference in the time of investment to serve new customers and the time when they connect to the system and pay their incremental-cost-pricing system-development charge.

A simplified illustration of these present-worth principles is shown in Table 3-3. In this example, a total investment of $2 600 000 is currently required for backup plant facilities to serve new customers. The utility has calculated that, based on the net revenue available for servicing investment capital, it can invest $1 020 000 for these customers. The utility projects that it will add 2000 new equivalent customers over the next five-year planning period. Thus, the incremental investment cost that will be derived from system-development charges equals the $1 580 000 difference between total investment cost and the amount supported by revenue. This equates to a $790 system-development charge per equivalent customer in the first year. An 8-percent interest rate is used to adjust this

Table 3-3 Illustration of Flow Funds Related to Incremental-Cost Pricing in Determining System-Development Charges

Total investment in backup facilities required		\$2 600 000
Less:		
Amount of investment that revenue stream will support		1 020 000
Incremental investment to be derived from SDC charges		\$1 580 000
Projected number of new equivalent ⅝-in. customers		2 000
SDC per equivalent customer		\$ 790
SDC charges required reflecting time value of money at 8% annual interest rate		
Year 1	\$790	
Year 2	853	
Year 3	921	
Year 4	995	
Year 5	1075	

first-year \$790 calculated system-development charge for subsequent years to reflect the time value of money.

System-development charges should reflect construction-cost-level changes occurring between the time when the charge is first determined and the charge is made. The intent is that the system-development charge be equal to the required investment if the construction were to occur at the time of contribution. Thus, charges should be adjusted periodically for price-level changes to match, as nearly as possible, the changes in construction-cost levels. For the example shown in Table 3-3, it was assumed that construction would be complete and paid for during the first year. If construction does not occur until a later year in the five-year cycle, the cost would have to be adjusted for any construction-cost-level changes.

Also, when a system-development charge is made before construction has started, the amount of this charge may have to be adjusted downward to reflect the time value of money between when the utility actually expends funds for the required plant facilities and when it received payment of the system-development charge. The interest rate at which the utility can earn on these funds could be used for this adjustment.

Once the total contribution level for new customers has been determined, a fee schedule for individual customers would be developed. With a base of ⅝-in.-connection customers having similar water-use characteristics, equivalent larger-size system-development charges could be designed reflecting applicable water-use and cost characteristics as well as differences in the size of the connection and meter. Data related to existing system investment, system capacity, customer data, projected water-use requirements, and customer base would have to be compiled and records maintained so that needed data could be retrieved as required. Also, adequate planning studies related to projected system growth, expected costs, and timing for necessary capital improvements would have to be prepared.

For water utilities serving areas with substantial new-customer growth, the incremental-cost pricing method is a sound way to determine a fair development charge for new customers. In contrast to the system buy-in method, it more nearly reflects the cost of adding new customers. In establishing contribution levels by this method, the long-run destabilizing effect of large-customer growth can be reduced or avoided to the benefit of both existing and new customers. Furthermore, this method tends to give the proper indication as to the actual cost of added system growth for new customers.

UTILITY EXTENSION REFUND POLICIES

Normally, investor-owned water utilities and some government-owned utilities have a refund provision for each customer connecting to a water-main extension made under rules requiring the applicant or developer to advance the cost of the extension. Rule 4.9 in

Table 3-4 Calculation of Main Extension Refund*

Utility rates at projected-use level for new single-family residential customer will produce annual revenue of			
General water use	$185		
Fire service	20		$205
Deduct costs of serving new customer			
Operating and maintenance expenses and taxes		$115	
Depreciation expense		30	145
Net revenues available to service investment			$ 60
At 11.75% rate of return this revenue will support an investment of			$510
Less: New customer's share of investment in backup facilities			310
Amount utility can invest in distribution mains and subject to refund			$200

*For a detailed discussion of how a main extension refund can be calculated see Woods, C.E. Principles of Discounting for Main Extensions. *Jour. AWWA*, 57:4:397 (Apr. 1965).

Appendix A illustrates this type of provision. The justification for a refund is that many water utilitys' rates are set so that revenue provides a return on the portion of the investment in distribution mains made by the utility.

The amount of the refunds and procedures for making them are governed by the rules and regulations under which the utility operates, as promulgated by its regulatory agency or policy-making body. Two examples of alternative procedures for calculating the amount of refund are given in the following paragraphs. In one example, a schedule of refund amounts for each class of customer having similar operating, revenue, and cost characteristics is calculated. In the other, a formula using the ratio of revenue to cost is used.

Refund Provisions

In the example shown in Table 3-4, the projected gross water revenues to be derived from a new customer are calculated based on the estimated use for a single-family residential customer. Each class of customer would require a separate analysis of operating, revenue, and cost data in the development of a refund amount for that class. From this gross revenue, the operating and maintenance expenses, taxes, and annual depreciation expenses required to serve the customer are deducted. The balance is the net revenue available to service the capital investment that the utility can make. Using the allowed rate of return of 11.75 percent, as used in this example, a gross investment of $510, which the net revenue would support, was calculated. Subtracted from this total investment is the customer's share in the backup plant facilities, which will be assigned to serve this customer's needs. In the example, $310 was used and deducted from the total supportable investment of $510, giving $200 as the amount that the utility could invest in distribution mains. Thus, the amount to be refunded from the total customer advance of capital made by the applicant would be $200.

As an alternative, some rate engineers have suggested that a formula could be used to determine the amount of the refund to be made to each new customer. Under this type of procedure, as illustrated in Table 3-5, it is assumed that all customers have the same operating, revenue, and cost characteristics and, therefore, one formula would be acceptable for all new customers. Where there are marked differences between individual customers or classes of customers, a more equitable refund will result if a separate calculation is made reflecting these differences when such differences have a significant impact on the amount to be refunded. A large user with markedly different operating characteristics than those of a single-family residential customer may require a relatively higher or lower refund, depending on how these characteristics impact the relationship of revenue and cost.

Table 3-5 Formula for Refund of Portion of Customer Advance for Construction Under Extension of Main Rules

Formula:

$$R = \frac{A - (A \times B/C)}{F} \times \frac{D}{E}$$

Where:

	Amount Used for This Example
R = Amount to be refunded	
A = Annual revenue from new customer	\$ 205
B = Utility operating revenue deductions	\$ 29 700 000
C = Utility operating revenues	\$ 42 000 000
D = Net investment in distribution mains	\$ 54 000 000
E = Total net utility plant investment	\$138 000 000
F = Utility's allowed rate of return	11.75%

Calculation:

$$R = \frac{\$205 - \left[\$205 \times \dfrac{29\ 700\ 000}{42\ 000\ 000}\right]}{0.1175} \times \frac{54\ 000\ 000}{138\ 000\ 000}$$

$$R = \frac{\$205 - (\$205 \times 0.707)}{0.1175} \times 0.39$$

$$R = \frac{\$205 - 145}{0.1175} \times 0.39$$

$$R = \$200$$

Note: For a detailed explanation in the derivation of this formula see Novaro, J.A. Financing Water Main Extensions in Connecticut. *Managing Water Rates and Finances—An AWWA Management Resource Book.* AWWA, Denver, Colo. (1979).

Some utilities have used procedures for a refund that are based on "free footage" or a multiple of revenue. These rules of thumb may or may not be appropriate for determining an equitable refund amount. Before they are used, a careful analysis of all data and costs should be made to document whether the rule produces the desired equitable results.

GOVERNMENT GRANTS AND LOW INTEREST LOANS

Another financing option that may be available for some water utilities is government grants or below-market-rate-interest loans. Both could reduce system-development charges and/or the cost of debt service that must come from the revenue stream, and thus, cut the cost to serve new customers.

At this time, federal aid for water utility construction is virtually nonexistent. Loan procedures are available to a limited extent at the federal level, but are becoming a priority in several states. Recent state-enacted programs provide a system of advancing loans at favorable interest rates by relying on the improved credit worthiness and/or borrowing capacity of the state agency versus the local agency. In some cases, interest rates may be subsidized. The general arrangement is to require a user-charge-supported system under which principal and interest are repaid to the funding agency to perpetuate the program on a revolving basis. In addition to requiring repayment through the proceeds from the sale of water, these newer state programs may also impose operating and planning requirements. Interconnections with adjacent systems to eliminate or reduce capital expenditures may be mandated. Overall water-supply management goals and objectives may require a more expensive system to be developed or even an existing supply to be replaced. Capital contributions by local agencies or cost-responsibility assignment by the state agency may be required to establish equitably the ultimate user charges to support the capital expenditure.

The administrative and regulatory process and requirements of a government grant program may create substantial additional costs to the utility that would exceed any benefit to be derived from acceptance of the grant. Requirements as to size of the plant, construction standards, labor rates, operating procedures, or other regulations can be overly restrictive and add to the cost of the plant and/or cause time delays. The result from related added-cost effects may create situations in which the utility would be better off to reject the use of government aid. Each situation must be studied carefully to ensure that the benefits to the system justify the added costs associated with receiving government aid.

Another consideration relating to the use of government grants or subsidized low-interest loans is that they expand the cost burden by shifting responsibility from the customer receiving service to a national or state base and from the user of the service to a nonuser. They can, in this context, provide a means to implement an overall policy that would, if fully paid by the utility, simply impose too great a cost burden on a specific group of customers. They may even provide a means to install water systems that would not be financially viable if the revenue derived had to support the full investment.

Over time, a serious revenue shortfall may result. Initially, the customers being served do not meet the current costs of receiving service because the revenues do not support the portion of the plant that was built through the grant or subsidization. Consequently, when the system or even a portion of the system needs to be replaced, the customers being served at that time can be subjected to major rate increases to cover the new investment. Responsibility has been shifted from one generation of customer to another, and the initial system that may not have been financially viable without a grant once again becomes a nonfeasible enterprise. To the extent that customers will support a level of rates and revenues that will provide funds to be set aside for this replacement process, this problem can be avoided. Even if a substantial portion of the plant is funded from grant money or financed by low-interest loans, the level of rates should be set sufficiently high so that as the plant wears out, the revenues needed to support a future bond issue to finance the plant replacement are available without large disruptive rate increases.

One caution in the use of government grants and loans is the fact that a government-owned system may have charter or state constitutional problems with acceptance of such grants and loans because borrowing may be limited to general obligation or revenue bonds requiring approval by the electorate.

Chapter 4

Ancillary Charges

In recent years, there has been an acceleration in the trend for water utilities to "unbundle" some of the ancillary services for producing water and require the user to pay for these services through separate fees and charges. Several factors have justified this trend.

With greater emphasis on equitability in the rate-setting process, any practice that improves matching revenues with cost enhances equity. The use of ancillary charges tends to increase operating efficiency by discouraging excessive, unnecessary, and wasteful demand for ancillary services by the customer.

As general water rates increase because of inflation, new plant requirements, and more stringent water-quality standards, policy makers and management view ancillary charges as a way of reducing general rate increases. The combination of fairness and improved efficiency makes ancillary charges an attractive way in which increased costs can be managed with the least impact on most customers. The ancillary charge is a refinement and expansion in the use of a cost-of-service methodology.

This chapter examines the following: (1) common types of ancillary charges used in the water utility industry (not all charges are applicable to all water utility operations), (2) when and under what circumstances a particular charge may be appropriate for an individual utility, and (3) some potential problems in the use of certain types of charges. Each utility must determine what types of charges are appropriate to its operations. By being aware of special problem areas, a utility can ensure that the benefit of using a particular charge will be achieved without creating problems in the operation and management of the utility.

USES OF ANCILLARY CHARGES

Ancillary charges normally are used only where the costs and revenues are significant, where the class of user is readily identifiable, and where the unit of use and its cost can be determined with reasonable accuracy. For example, if 30 percent of a utility's customer base is responsible for 80 percent of account changes in a year (this might occur in a college town where there is a large student population changing their residence each year) and the cost is significant to the utility's operation, then it may be appropriate to have a customer-transfer charge to recoup these costs. The revenues from the costs associated with the use of ancillary charges should be reflected in the overall cost-of-service study used by the utility in developing its total-revenue requirements.

It would not be appropriate to charge for a service if the service affects the quality of water or the integrity of treatment processes. For example, a utility would want to respond to reports of taste, odor, or color problems as quickly as possible to determine the cause and take corrective action. A utility would not want to discourage customer reports of this nature by charging for the cost of investigations. This type of service call does benefit more than one customer and can aid the utility in ensuring that the source of a problem does not affect other customers. The same principle applies in reporting leaks. Leaks may cause property or personal damage that could result in a lawsuit against the utility. In situations of this nature, the utility must weigh the problem of the small percentage of customers who "cry wolf" at any sign of a service problem against the value of encouraging customers to report real problems. Pressure tests, restoration of water service due to breaks in the utility's facilities, leak-detection programs, and similar activities that affect service and safety for all customers are normally associated with furnishing general water service and are paid for through the water-rate structure of the utility.

Other factors to consider in the use of ancillary charges would be legislative, legal, and regulatory constraints under which the utility is required to operate. Before ancillary charges can be incorporated into a rate structure, the utility must be sure that they are acceptable to its regulators and comply with legislative mandates. The utility must ensure that when revenue projections are developed for ancillary charges, overly optimistic levels of use and revenue are not anticipated with the result that required levels of total revenue are not achieved. This is especially true for services where fixed costs are involved. To encourage reasonable uses of a service, ancillary charges must have a direct relationship to a unit of use, be large enough to justify their use, and be of sufficient magnitude to impact the user decision-making process.

Whether a particular type of ancillary charge is used by an individual utility will depend on its policy objectives and operating characteristics. Certain types of charges, such as jobbing and merchandise sales, do have universal acceptance in the industry. When such services are provided by the utility, they are normally charged directly to the individual customer. Fees may be imposed when the activity is normally provided only to a small group of customers and would impose extraordinary costs on all rate payers if not charged separately.

Sound management practice dictates that both government-owned and investor-owned water utilities maintain a good public image, and community understanding is essential in the process of securing support for new bond authorizations and/or general water-rate increases. Ancillary charges are not intended to overburden new or existing customers with a proliferation of different charges and operating rules and regulations. Recovery of all conceivable capital and operating-cost overheads is not the objective of these kinds of charges. While the relative magnitude of ancillary charges should be established for the circumstances unique to each utility's operations, accepted water utility practices must also be considered and applied to the identification, design, and administration of these charges.

The use of a fixed-fee schedule, rather than billing the actual cost incurred for a particular service, is a practice that is receiving acceptance in the industry. Where the administrative costs of determining individual charges are greater than can be justified by the differential in what would be charged over a fixed-fee rate, such schedules of charges are justified. Also, where there is little difference between the average cost of a service and the high or low cost, the use of a fixed-fee schedule is obviously justified.

There are a variety of ancillary charges in the water utility industry that can be developed. Examples cover collection and delinquency charges, turn-on and turn-off fees, various application fees, tapping charges, and jobbing and merchandising sales. When special charges are used, the utility should coordinate these rates and charges with its customer-service section. Procedures must be developed to ensure that the customer has advance warning about services that will trigger a charge. Billing procedures must be in place to properly account for special charges. Bill inserts and other forms of customer notification are effective tools for keeping customers informed. As with all utility operations, a well-developed training program is a solid foundation on which good public relations can be built. Customer-service personnel must have all necessary information available so that they can explain the intent and circumstances to which each charge applies. This will go far in avoiding the perception that these charges are punitive and will enhance the utility's effort to promote goodwill.

WATER FEES AND CHARGES ASSESSED AGAINST PROPERTY

In the case of most government-owned water utilities, water service is furnished to the property and fees are charged to the property owner. Provisions in the legislation that enable the operation of government-owned utilities will normally contain language similar to the following:

> "Such rates or charges, if not paid when due, shall constitute a lien upon the premises served and a past-due charge shall bear interest at the same rate as would unpaid taxes."

Normally, the legislation will specify that bills must be paid within a specified number of days or the lien provisions become operative. Appropriate utility officials are authorized to record liens in the public records of the governmental unit, with the cost of recording being added to unpaid water charges and interest. All charges must be paid in full before the lien is released.

In some regulatory jurisdictions, the investor-owned water utility is permitted to hold the property owner responsible for water bills. However, most regulatory agencies do not permit this practice. When permitted, regulators will normally prescribe the procedures to be used by the utility so that both the utility and customer are protected.

Utilities with this type of provision may bill the tenant or occupant of the premises for water charges at the request of the owner, expressed or implied, but this does not relieve the property owner from the responsibility for payment of all outstanding charges.

When a utility holds the property owner responsible for payment of water bills, it must develop effective procedures to ensure that the property owner is kept informed as to the status of the account when it becomes delinquent or when a tenant leaves with an unpaid balance. Often a property owner may be able to offset amounts outstanding against rent deposits in order to prevent tenants from avoiding unpaid obligations. Good communications and public relations between the property owner and utility about changes in tenant status will result in timely billings and speed up the payment/collection process.

Field-Service Charges

Some of the more common types of field-service charges and fees relate to activities associated with water turn on (or off), meter setting or removal, special meter readings, meter testing, and temporary hydrant meter settings. Each type of charge has its place in the rate-setting process for certain operational conditions. As previously mentioned, these charges would be used only where there is a customer group that can be identified, where the activity produces significant costs that are not common to all customers, and where costs can be identified and related to the units of activity so that a charge or fee for the service can be developed. The subsections that follow describe some of the common types of field-service charges.

Turn-on/turn-off fees. A utility may charge to turn on or turn off water service. Turn-on charges are very common because they are easy to administer and collect. Turn-off charges are not usually made because utilities have found it important that the customer report when service is to be discontinued. This enables the utility to remove the meter or take other necessary actions to avoid waste or illegal uses. When turn-off charges are made, emergency turn-offs are normally exempted.

The turn-on charge can be imposed for new-service turn on, seasonal turn ons or other situations where the service is temporarily discontinued for operating-rule and/or engineering-standard violations, or when delinquent accounts have been shut off. The utility may add a surcharge for turn-ons completed at night or after office hours in order to compensate for the shift pay differential. Many utilities incorporate all routine turn-on activities into one turn-on charge when the cost differential between various activities does not justify separate fees or when the cost of administering a complex fee structure is greater than the benefit. Included in the cost of turn-on or turn-off activities would be personnel travel time to the customer's premises, actual labor costs involved in operation of the curb valve, use of equipment, and appropriate overhead costs associated with the activity.

Field-collection charge. Utility service personnel often are permitted to collect delinquent water bills at the customer's premises, especially if such payments are not in cash. When a delinquent payment is made to the service personnel who goes to the customer's premises for the purpose of shutting off the water, the service fee can be reduced because the cost is less than the normal turn-off fee, provided suspension-of-service actions did not commence. This type of collection policy can significantly reduce the number of turn-offs, thereby reducing the work load for office and field-service personnel and improving customer relations. The customer benefits from uninterrupted service, a smaller service charge, and avoids the inconvenience of traveling to the utility office to pay the delinquent bill. Such a policy also eliminates the need to impose a bill-collector fee, except in the most difficult cases.

However, some large urban utilities have reconsidered the benefits of on-premise collection because of problems that sometimes occur when collectors or field personnel confront delinquent customers who are unwilling to pay.

Illegal turn-ons. On occasion, a customer will turn a service back on illegally and, in the process, make the stop box inoperative. In this case, the utility should instruct the customer to take corrective measures within a prescribed period of time or the utility should send a field-service crew to clean out or dig up the stop box so that the service can be shut off until the matter is remedied. Normally, a uniform fee plus a higher charge is imposed, but only where it is necessary to dig up and/or replace the stop box.

Routine clean-outs and dig-ups of stop boxes and/or meter pits are sometimes undertaken by the utility without a separate charge to the customer. This occurs where the special service is not a result of illegal customer activity and is justified because utilities have found that quick access to these boxes benefit the system as a whole.

Special meter readings/final readings. A fee may be charged when customers request a special meter reading or ask that a meter be reread even though, in the opinion of the utility, no reading is warranted. The charge is designed to recover the higher-than-normal cost of this reading. For example, a customer may feel that the meter reading is in error and request that it be read again. To prevent abuse of this service, a utility may charge for a second reading under certain conditions. If a substantial reading discrepancy is found or if the individual customer seldom demands this service, it is common practice for the utility not to make a charge. The definition of "an excessive number of requests" varies with each utility, but one standard might be that no more than one such request is made during a calendar year. A meter-reading charge is usually a fixed fee based on historical costs for performing special readings.

A final-bill reading is a common type of special reading. This may occur when a home or business is sold, leased, and/or vacated, or when a new owner/customer occupies the premises. Final readings are usually recorded by service personnel rather than meter readers because the request for a specific day or time seldom coincides with the scheduled day of a specific meter route. The final meter-reading charge can take the form of a uniform fee, which is added to the final billing statement. The charge recovers the meter-reading cost plus additional clerical costs for issuing the final statement.

Meter size change. When a customer with an existing service and meter, such as a 1-in. service line with a ⅝-in. or ¾-in. meter, wants the meter changed to a larger size, the customer may be required to pay the increased cost of the meter and the cost of installation. This is a special situation where customers, for their convenience, want a larger meter installed but where the utility does not deem that the change is necessary. In instances where the customer's use pattern has changed (increased) and a larger service line has been installed (at the customer's expense) and where such use requires a larger meter, the customer would pay on the basis of the regular rates of the utility. If, as is the case for many utilities, there is a charge for the meter and its installation, this would form the basis for the charge. A meter-size-change fee is designed to discourage changes where, in the judgment of the utility, such a change is not needed.

Installation of remote meter-reading devices. Some utilities will provide, for the convenience of the customer, an outside remote meter-reading device in areas where a meter is normally installed inside the premises. When this is a special service and not available to all customers, a charge may be made. The fee may be a one-time charge or it may be spread over a period of months (with appropriate interest charged, similar to a level-pay mortgage schedule) so that the customer avoids having to make a large up-front payment.

Meter resetting fee. A charge may be made to a customer for resetting a meter when the meter was removed at the request of the customer. Normally, this charge will vary with the size of the meter. It may be combined with a turn-on charge where both meter set and service turn-on are performed at the same time.

Appointment charge. In certain instances, a customer may request a field-service call at a specified time during the working day. A field-appointment charge is often made for the added cost of making a service call at a specific time. The cost could include the added travel time because of the disruption to the field representative's scheduled work activity.

Meter testing charge. High-water-bill complaints that are not resolved by telephone may necessitate that a meter be reread or a leak inspection be made of the customer's service line or water-using appliances. If the matter is not resolved to the customer's satisfaction, then the meter may be removed and tested at the request of the customer. If the field-service representative suspects that the meter has become inaccurate, a test may be ordered at the utility's expense. A meter removed and bench tested at the request of the customer and found to be accurate can be subject to a fixed fee reflecting the average removal and testing costs for that particular meter size or type. As an alternative, some utilities may require the customer to make a deposit to cover the actual cost of the test. If the meter meets the utility's standards, the deposit is used to pay the cost; if the meter tests outside of these standards, the deposit is returned to the customer. With investor-owned utilities, the requirements of the regulatory agency will be reflected in the procedures that are followed.

Financial responsibility for meters that test outside of the prescribed accuracy range will depend on the maintenance and replacement policy of the individual utility. Payment for replacement of the meter also will depend on these policies, with some utilities requiring the meter to be replaced by the customer and others making replacement at the utility's expense.

Temporary hydrant permit. Nonfire-related water uses from public fire hydrants, such as street washing, dust control, lawn service, and tank truck filling, are normally allowed, provided the applicant first obtains a special permit from the water utility. Amounts charged for the hydrant permit can include the office and field costs for administering and monitoring the metered or unmetered connection, in addition to a provision for the actual or estimated water use resulting from the activity. Many water utilities prefer to carefully control and meter these generally limited activities and will initially charge a uniform fee that provides for a minimum-base water-use allowance. Metered water use in excess of the base allowance becomes subject to the general retail water rates, thereby adding to the final hydrant-permit cost. A separate and refundable deposit for the rental meter and hydrant wrench is normally set at an amount sufficient to assure their safe return. Inspections are usually required to ensure that these uses meet all utility operating standards, and the cost of inspection is normally included in the fee.

Office-Service Charges

Some of the more common types of office-service charges include the cost of collecting delinquent accounts, the added cost of setting up a new account or transferring an existing account, or the cost associated with checks that are returned by the bank for insufficient funds. Some of these activities include initial office activities, and if these activities are unsuccessful, follow-up field work may be necessary.

New account or transfer charge. Depending on the level of activity and overall costs, an initial administrative fee may be charged a new applicant for the average costs incidental to opening a new account or transferring an existing account. Such fees will directly reimburse the utility for the cost of additional utility services that may be performed before the new or existing service becomes active or is reactivated.

Fees will reflect the status of the service connection. If the service connection is already established, the transfer fee can be designed to recover the office-related costs for completing the application form, determining the applicant's credit rating and/or nonproperty owner's water-use-related deposit, collection of any unpaid water bills or assessments, and any other activities preliminary to instituting water service. Most government-owned utilities do not require a credit investigation because the water charges usually are considered under the applicable state or local laws as a lien against the property. When water-suspension policies require that the water be left disconnected and where the stop box and/or water meter already is installed on the customer's premises, any additional office and field costs for initiating the turn-on order can also be incorporated into this charge.

An account fee for new construction can incorporate the additional office expenses incurred for administering any special capital-cost payments (discussed in Chapter 1). The fee can also be used to cover the cost of administering and monitoring the new service line during the construction phase.

An administrative fee can be used to pay the added cost of reprocessing a new water-service cancellation, which results in a refund of any capital-cost payments or other deposits (water-main extension, tapping fee, or connection charges) previously paid in connection with the issuance of a new license or permit. This fee can be deducted from the refund and the net balance returned to the licensee or applicant.

Whether one fee is used for all activities or separate fees are developed will depend on the amount of activity and the cost differential between fees. Efficiency in the administration of a fee program must be considered when determining each fee.

Collection-related charges. The service fees discussed in the following paragraphs pertain principally to the collection and billing functions of the water utility. Because most relate to the collection of delinquent water bills, each should be reviewed periodically to see if changes in the utility's overall collection program can reduce the number of unpaid bills and provide better control over these activities.

Delinquency fee. A late-payment delinquency fee can be an incentive for prompt payment. This essentially recognizes the time value of money and other added costs incurred. It is common practice for a water utility to designate a period of time during which a bill must be paid to avoid delinquency fees. Many utilities use 15 days, with a three-day grace period to reflect any mail delivery problems, before collection procedures are initiated. A utility will normally coordinate office and field work to shorten the length of time an account is delinquent and minimize the amount of effort required to collect payment.

Short-check charge. A charge is normally made when a check is not honored by the customer's bank, regardless of the reason. This generally reflects the added cost to the utility for processing a bad check. The charge may be a fixed fee or a percentage of the check. One utility has the following charge in its published rates: "Dishonored Check . . . $10.00 or 5 percent of the check amount, whichever is greater."

The fee may also include the added costs for the cashier department, commercial division, and telephone or letter notices. When a customer has a sustained record of bad checks, the utility may require a deposit account until a good credit rating is reestablished. When checks are not made good within a prescribed period, the utility may initiate service shut-off since the account is actually delinquent.

With investor-owned utilities, the requirements of the regulatory agency must be reflected in the policies, procedures, and charges. All policies are usually required to be filed with the regulatory agency.

Jobbing and Merchandise Sales

A service charge is common when the utility performs work on the customer's premises (jobbing repairs, replacement, improvements, etc.) or sells merchandise to the customer or the plumber who will install the merchandise. In recent years, charges have been expanded to include the installation of lawn-irrigation systems and backflow-prevention devices for customers. Some utilities even provide financing to the customer for such services and allow the customer to pay the cost over a period of time as an addition to the regular water bill. The utility can usually charge for these services at a higher rate of interest than it pays and still provide a service to the customer at a cost savings over commercial interest rates. However, only where adequate protection against bad debts can be designed into the system is this practice prudent (for example, where the utility can place a lien on the property to ensure collection).

The utility may find itself in competition with local plumbing contractors, and this must be taken into consideration in determining what level of work the utility will undertake. Where there is little competition among contractors, the utility can be a means of ensuring that a fair and competitive price is developed and that the customer receives the best service possible. By setting installation standards and acting as an alternative to do the work, the utility can provide benefits to the customer.

A special fee schedule can be developed for installation of backflow-prevention devices, or the utility may want to charge individual customers on the basis of the actual cost. If the average cost of the installation does not vary too greatly from extreme costs (high or low), then a fee schedule may be used. If the customer is charged a jobbing fee based on cost, the utility should insist on an advance deposit based on its estimate of the final cost of the work.

Some activities that a utility might undertake through its jobbing and contract-work programs would include

- service-line repairs,
- meter and remote-reader repairs,
- replacement and/or enlargement of services,
- material sales to customers and/or plumbers,
- repair to customer's water-using appliances, and
- sales of meters when the customer is required to provide the meter at his/her own expense.

The extent to which a utility offers these services will depend on local conditions and customs. If participation by the water utility will benefit its customers, these activities may be considered. Adequate planning and costing techniques must be part of the process to ensure that these activities do pay all direct and indirect associated costs.

Tapping Charges

Most utilities have a set schedule for installing taps into the main when connecting to customer service lines. When a customer or customer's plumber applies for a tap, the fee is collected based on the size of the tap needed to make the service connection. When large taps are required or special costs are involved (such as a large tap into a reinforced concrete main), the utility may require that the payment reflect the added costs. If so, at the time of application, a determination would be made and the customer/applicant charged accordingly. Included in these charges would be the costs for any permanent repairs to the pavement, which normally would be completed at a later date.

If a premises is demolished and the tap is disconnected from the main, there may be a charge made to the property owner. Because of the difficulty in collecting for such work, it is standard practice, where possible, to put a lien against the property and permit no future tapping to serve the property until the cost of the tap cutoff has been paid. Normally, a physical cutoff is not required for services that will not undergo any modification or replacement and where the owner can show that water service will be restored within a reasonable time. Regulatory requirements must be considered by investor-owned utilities in charging for a physical disconnection of service. Office and field costs should be included in the charge made for service-tap cutoffs since there can be a substantial cost to the utility in record keeping.

Special Meter Rates

When a utility provides service for a large, wholesale customer, a special rate may be charged to pay for added costs necessary to serve the customer. As an alternative, the utility may require that the customer furnish, install, and maintain, at the customer's expense, all special facilities (meters, valves, fittings, meter pit, etc.) that may be required to provide the service. The justification for this charge is that special facilities normally are not included in the general rates for water service because of the substantial variation in cost from one customer to another. The customer benefiting from the installation should pay all additional maintenance and capital costs associated with the installation so that other customers do not have to assume the burden of these costs. Capital contributions and special meter rates using a demand contract, where appropriate, or a combination of both (see Chapter 1) are ways in which the utility can prevent this.

Application, Engineering, and Inspection Fees

There are many types of application, engineering, and inspection fees used in the water utility industry. Some are designed to recover only the direct costs associated with certain customer activities. Others are designed to recover both the direct overhead costs of processing the application and some of the indirect costs incurred when determining the background data required to process new applications for service. For example, if the utility must expend funds for an engineering study that will ensure that expansion into a new area can be undertaken, a portion of this cost might be added to new-application fees. As an alternative, these costs may be included as part of system-development charges.

Since costs are incurred to process an application even where no work is ultimately performed, the utility is justified in requiring that applicants making preliminary inquiries pay the costs associated with the work. If no construction is undertaken, then costs must be absorbed either by other applicants who do commit for work or by general water-service customers. A nominal preliminary-application fee can help to deter unnecessary inquiries and pay costs when they do not result in construction.

The level of application fees will vary and, as with all service charges, should be based on a cost analysis of those activities required to process the application. Direct administrative costs for personnel handling the application, engineering services used, field-service needs, and other related activities should all be determined and a fee structure developed based on the level of activity. A description of some of the more common types of application and inspection fees follows.

Main inspection, filing, and contract fees. A fee may be charged for filing the application, developing the contract, and for field inspection and engineering record reviews necessary when preparing an extension-of-main agreement. The flat fee would be paid at the time the application is received, and the fee would be applied towards the cost of the work at the time the contract for an extension is signed. If no work is undertaken, then the application fee is retained by the utility to defray costs of administrative activities. Nonrefundable initial administrative flat filing fees are required from each applicant by some utilities.

Administrative fee for service-connection inspection. Where a new service-line stub-in is connected to the distribution system before service is actually required, a fee may be charged to defray the cost of administering and monitoring the new connection. Once water service begins, the account can then be transferred to permanent status.

Cross-connection inspection. A periodic-inspection fee for high-risk installations to ensure that no cross connection has occurred is used to recover costs associated with such inspections. The utility would couple this fee with its overall cross-connection-control program, including adequate records of installations, periodic scheduling of inspections, and regulations sufficient to ensure that infractions will be corrected promptly to avoid possible contamination of the system.

Engineering-design fee. Where substantial engineering design and study are required to provide new facilities for an applicant's water-service requirements, the extraordinary engineering service cost may also be charged to the applicant, over and above the administrative fee. This can be charged either as a flat fee or on an actual-cost basis, with a deposit of the estimated cost being required in advance of the work being undertaken. Often an extension of service requires engineering work to determine what additional facilities (mains, distribution storage, pumping, etc.) will be required, and frequently such facilities must be designed and plans and contracts prepared. Such extraordinary costs benefiting only the individual applicant/developer should be assessed against the property owner.

If the facilities are actually constructed, such costs may be capitalized as part of the total construction cost of the extension of service, and the amount received becomes part of the customer-contributed capital for the project. Where no work is undertaken (the project is abandoned), the funds received are accounted for in accordance with the utility's system of accounts. The expenses incurred are charged against revenues. With a sound cost-estimating program, the revenue and expenses should be equal, and the cost will not be borne by the utility and its general service customers. If overall systems planning is necessary for development of an area in the utility's system, a planning fee may also be assessed against the developer of the area for which plans are designed.

Construction-Water Charges

A water charge may be assessed and collected at the time the contractor initiates a new tap application and requires water for construction purposes. Water is normally supplied through a service line that, depending on policy, can either be temporarily metered or unmetered before the permanent meter is set.

Where it is practical to meter water use, the construction-water charge will be based on the general water rates applicable to the particular retail water service. Any initial deposit would be applied toward the total water charges calculated at the termination of the temporary permit or construction period.

Because of potential abuses, relative small usage volumes, high building activity, and other factors, it is often more practical and cost effective to bill for construction water on an unmetered basis, particularly if there is a large number of residential projects under construction. Field checks for illegal jumpers in place of the meters, reversed or stolen meters, and subsequent attempts to recover unauthorized water-use charges can be avoided with an unmetered flat-fee approach. Typically, a fixed-fee schedule can be designed by increasing the fee with the size of connection (i.e., ⅝-in. and/or ¾-in., 1-in., 1½-in., etc. meter-connection sizes). The fixed-fee schedule also should be based on utility studies for the actual metered average use experienced during construction for each individual connection or grouping of connection sizes and resulting revenue levels that would have been experienced had meters been installed. Studies may show that the additional costs for installing and monitoring a construction meter or attempting to detect and collect for illegal unmetered uses is not economically justified even for the larger connection sizes.

Miscellaneous Work

Often a developer will provide a development map with elevations that subsequently are changed. Consequently, it will be necessary to raise, lower, or even move mains, fire hydrants, meter boxes, service lines, or backflow preventers. These relocation costs, which are the result of the builder's actions, are normally paid for by the developer. The utility will usually require advance payment for the work and will withhold service to the property until the facilities meet with the utility's operating/construction standards. A deposit from the developer is usually required. After the actual cost is determined, the final bill is adjusted.

Unauthorized Water Use

When use without a permit and without payment of applicable fees is discovered at a metered or unmetered construction site or customer's premises, an additional charge may be imposed for unauthorized water use. As a deterrent to future abuses, the unauthorized-water-use charge can be set at a level equal to what would have been paid had the use been authorized, together with an additional amount necessary to recover any additional cost of detection and collection. In most water systems, separate fees for illegal removals or damage to seals on the meter, stop box, fire-detector check, etc. are added to the unauthorized-water-use charge.

Unit Cost Development

If a utility does not have the accounting capacities necessary to develop cost data for each activity for which a charge is to be made, a time-and-material study can be used to determine the average cost for various activities. These standard time-and-material studies can be the basis for developing fees for the activities. Where the cost differential between activities does not warrant a separate fee, groups of activities may be combined and a standard rate can be charged. To the extent that the utility can simplify its system of charges within the constraint of cost-based charges, it can reduce the administrative costs involved in operating its ancillary-charge system.

Accounting records can be used as a checklist to ensure that all costs associated with a project (direct and indirect overheads) are reflected in the cost study prepared to form the basis for a particular fee or charge. Although historical costs will have to be adjusted to reflect any price-level changes (changes in labor rates, material prices, overhead allocations, etc.), such costs can give valuable information regarding normal material and labor usages. They can also show when costs for various activities indicate a marked differential so that separate fees may be designed to reflect this. Thus, a good accounting system is a valuable tool for managing the affairs of the utility.

Both investor- and government-owned utilities must guard against overly optimistic estimates of use and revenue from miscellaneous charges. Otherwise, there could be a shortfall in revenue if the estimates are not representative of an "average" year and if the estimates do not reflect a reduced level of use associated with the full cost charge being made for services.

The procedures for calculating the unit costs used as the basis for charging for a particular activity will vary with each utility. One method is to make a time study on labor requirements (type of employee needed to perform the required activity, travel, and operation time), material needs, transportation, and other equipment uses as developed for the "average" task, using statistical sampling procedures. As an alternative, when the utility's operating and accounting records permit, the actual historical unit costs for the operations under study could be determined. These would be adjusted for price-level changes (or changes in operating requirements) for labor, materials, or equipment used. Both methods should include all appropriate overhead costs.

Under a time-study procedure, the utility would first identify those operations it would perform to complete the required service and those required to be done by the customer or the customer's plumber. Then a study of the time required for the utility to perform its tasks would be made for a sufficient number of operations in order to obtain a valid statistical sample. Added to this study would be the material and equipment requirements and the average time needed to travel to and from the job site. These units of labor, materials, and equipment would be priced at the utility's current prices including appropriate overheads. Unit costs are normally rounded to provide a fixed-fee schedule for various service sizes. For those job conditions that are not normal, an actual-cost price (with a deposit of the estimated cost paid in advance) may be used when the resulting projected costs exceed the average by a substantial amount.

As an example of how this price could be developed, the policies and procedures that resulted in the fee for a ¾-in. tap to a water utility's main follow:

- When applicable, the applicant (plumber) is responsible for obtaining a street-opening permit from the municipality. (In this instance, inspection of the closing of the excavation, temporary patch, and permanent patch are all done by the municipality with the cost included in the fee charged for the street-opening permit.)
- The applicant, at his/her expense, is responsible for the installation of the service connection in a prepared trench according to the specifications required by the utility.
- The utility taps its main and installs the corporation stop, connects the stop to the gooseneck on the service connection, and inspects the service line to ensure that it meets the utility's size, material, and installation requirements.
- On approval by the utility, the applicant backfills the trench and has the required temporary or permanent pavement repairs made as required.
- The utility's service personnel reports to operations on the status of the tap (size, location, etc.) for processing by engineering and customer-account personnel.
- Account personnel initiate inspection procedures to ensure that when the premises are occupied, a meter will be set and the account will become active for future billing purposes.

The estimated costs* to the utility may be as follows:

Application-processing labor	$ 8.00
Operation labor, including travel, installation, and inspection	60.00
Account-inspection labor	8.00
Material uses—corporation stop, etc.	12.00
Transportation and equipment	12.00
Total unit cost and fee	$100.00

*All costs include applicable overheads, and the term *service connection* is defined as a portion of the customer's service line from the main to the property line where a curb box and shut-off valve must be installed.

Some large utility systems use prior-year actual costs adjusted for changes in price for labor, materials, and equipment uses. The utility would do all of the work involved in tapping the main, installing the service connection from the main to the meter box, and installing the meter. This work includes excavation, connecting the customer's service line, restoring the street, and (when required) restoring the ground from the street to the meter box. The average cost for a ¾-in. meter installation for the prior year adjusted for a 6-percent labor-rate change and a 3-percent material-price increase would be as follows:

Labor, including all applicable overheads	$ 62.50
All materials and overheads*	68.50
Equipment uses and overheads	12.00
Total unit cost and fee	$143.00

*Materials would include the corporation stop, tubing, fittings, valves, meter, and meter box.

These examples illustrate the process of setting activity charges, but it should be explicitly understood that each water utility should carefully analyze its particular policies and operations in identifying the cost components that form the basis for making tap/meter installation charges.

CONCLUSION

Each utility operation, to a certain extent, is unique; therefore, the combination of charges that will best suit it must be developed on the basis of individual needs. These needs will change over time in a dynamic utility operation. The size of the customer base affected and the ability to identify individual users of the particular service are important factors in selecting a particular charge.

The significance of the revenue/cost/use pattern is also an important consideration. Since administrative costs can be an important part of any rate-setting process, the utility must be sure that the revenue generated by the activity and the related costs are large enough to justify processing the miscellaneous charges.

Finally, costs must be identifiable and related to a unit of use so that an appropriate rate or fee can be developed. To the extent that a utility has special ancillary charges as part of its overall rate-setting strategy, greater equity and better efficiency may be achieved.

Appendix A

Example of Rules, Regulations, and Rates Governing the Extension of Water Mains

I. DEFINITIONS

1.1 "Extension" shall mean the lineal footage of Main required in order to service property(ies) according to the terms and conditions set forth herein.

1.2 "Extension Contract" shall mean a contract executed by the Utility and the Applicant providing for the installation of an Extension pursuant to which the cost of such Extension is paid by the Applicant to the Utility. An Extension Contract may be either an Advance-Payment Extension Contract or a Deferred-Payment Extension Contract.

1.3 "Advance-Payment Extension Contract" shall mean an Extension Contract that provides for full payment by the Applicant in advance of construction as described in Section 4.1 of these rules.

1.4 "Deferred-Payment Extension Contract" shall mean an Extension Contract that provides for partial payment by the Applicant in advance of construction and deferred payment of the balance, together with interest, as described in Section 5.1 of these rules.

1.5 "Applicant" shall mean the party entering into a contract with the Utility for an Extension.

1.6 "Utility" shall mean the water system for which these rules apply.

1.7 "Taker" shall mean any party connected directly to an existing Extension by a service line on which an Extension Contract is in effect.

1.8 "Mains" are water pipes owned by or to be owned by the Utility used for the purpose of conveying water to Taker's service connections.

II. APPLICATIONS

2.1 Application for Extensions will be accepted only when filed by the owner of public record of the property that the Extension will serve.

2.2 Applications shall be made at the offices of the Utility on forms provided and will not be accepted until all information outlined on said forms is supplied.

2.3 Extensions will be made on streets that are accepted and maintained by the town or city or in rights-of-way granted to the Utility. Extension will also be made on new streets subject to the following: (a) the street shall be constructed to line and grade conforming to the plan and profile as accepted by and recorded with the town or city; (b) a bond has been posted with the town or city by the owner to ensure satisfactory completion of said street according to the specifications of the town or city, and that the town or city accept and maintain the new street as a town or city street; and (c) that all of the above be subject to written confirmation by the proper municipal authority.

2.4 Until a street has been accepted by the municipality, or in other private roadways, no new Mains will be installed until street line and grades are established, street is graded in a manner acceptable to the Utility, and until grants of rights-of-way have been given the Utility, at no expense to the Utility to install, maintain, extend, and replace Mains and appurtenances and make connections thereto in said street(s).

2.5 If requested by the Utility, the Applicant shall erect and maintain stakes to indicate correct street lines and grades to facilitate proper installation of the Mains.

2.6 The determination of the required length and size of an Extension shall, in all cases, be made by the Utility but, in general, shall be based on the following principles: (a) the terminal point of Extensions laid in streets not within a development shall be the property line beyond the last Taker to be served by the Extension; (b) if the Extension is laid in streets within a development or subdivision, it shall include all Mains required to cover houses to be served by the Extension plus any Main required to connect dead ends created within the development or subdivision at intersecting streets; and (c) the size of Main to be installed will be based on the existing and future needs of the Utility's water system, and the costs will be allocated as provided in Section 3.4 of these rules.

2.7 Application for the Extension of Main will be automatically cancelled 60 days from the date of application if, within this period, all conditions required for acceptance of such applications, as set forth in these rules, are not fulfilled.

2.8 On cancellation of an Extension application, the Applicant may renew said application. However, the renewed application will be subject to and governed by the rules in effect at the date of renewal.

2.9 Extensions will not be scheduled for construction until all conditions and contractual obligations herein set forth have been fully complied with by the Applicant for said Extension.

2.10 Extensions will normally be assigned for construction in the order in which all requirements as herein outlined have been met; however, the Utility may vary such assignment in order to integrate timing with other projects that may have been approved and are waiting for construction, and to take due consideration of weather conditions, availability of materials, and immediacy of need.

2.11 The Applicant, if a development is involved, will be required to furnish with the application one reproducible map of the property to be supplied, and it must be a facsimile of one approved and filed with the proper municipal authority. Applicant agrees to proceed with construction of the development in such a manner as to allow the Utility to construct the Extension continuously on a street-by-street basis.

2.12 If requested by the Utility, the Applicant shall furnish plan and profile of the street in which the Main is to be installed as approved by and filed with the municipality, which plan and profile shall show, in addition to the street grade as approved, existing grade at street corner line and each property line or at such other location as may be designated by the utility, giving the date at which the profile of said existing grade was made. Only maps, plans, profiles, or other drawings prepared and stamped by a licensed engineer or surveyor will be acceptable.

2.13 All requests for the installation of public fire hydrants shall be made directly to the municipality and shall be subject to order by said municipality.

2.14 If property to be supplied by an Extension is at such an elevation that, in the opinion of the Utility, adequate pressure cannot be furnished at all times, the Applicant for such an Extension will be obligated to execute a low-pressure agreement prior to final acceptance by the Utility of the application, which low-pressure agreement may be recorded at the option of the Utility in the land records of the municipality in which the property is situated.

2.15 The Application shall be accompanied by the application fee as prescribed in the Utility's rates and charges schedule.

III. GENERAL RULES

3.1 Title of ownership in an Extension shall at all times be and remain vested in the Utility.

3.2 An Extension shall at all times remain under the sole control and jurisdiction of the Utility. This includes the right to connect additional customers without the consent of the Applicant, make further Extensions beyond or running laterally from said Extension, or connect said Extension with any other portion of the distribution system of the Utility, without incurring any obligations to the Applicant or Takers receiving service from said Extension except as hereinafter provided.

3.3 When Main Extensions are made in unfinished street the Applicant shall be fully responsible for damages to the Main and all fixtures and appurtenances, such as hydrants, gate boxes, blowoff boxes, etc., including the location thereof, if such damage results from or such relocation is necessitated by acts of the Applicant or his/her agents. If, after the Mains are laid, the surface grade is lowered with the result that the required minimum cover of the Mains, fixtures, or appurtenances is not maintained, then the Applicant shall pay the cost of lowering the Mains to the level required to correct this deficiency. This responsibility shall remain in force until such time as the street is officially accepted by the proper municipal authority.

3.4 The Utility will determine the size of the Main required. Costs will normally be based on sizes not larger than an 8-in. Main, but if for any reason it is necessary to install Mains larger than 8 in. to satisfy requirements of the Applicant, cost shall be based on the cost of the Main size actually required. If larger than 8-in. Mains are installed to satisfy requirements of the utility, only the cost of installing 8-in. Mains will be charged to the Applicant. Cost for the purpose of all Extension Contracts shall be the actual cost of the Main, labor and equipment used, plus overheads at the prevailing Utility overhead rates for the Main size required. If pavement excavation and replacement or repairs are required for the Extension, the additional costs of the required excavation and replacement or repairs will be added to the cost of the Extension.

3.5 In cases where an Extension will pass by corner properties that have access to a Main on an adjacent street, the Utility will install, at its expense, that corner property's portion of the Extension from the existing Main to the far property line. If this distance is subdividable in accordance with the zoning regulations of the town or city where the Main Extension occurs, the Utility will only install, at its expense, the corner property's portion of the Extension from the existing Main to the subdivided line, but in no case will the distance contributed by the Utility exceed 150 ft. This policy will not apply to new developments where the corner lot costs will be absorbed by the entire development.

3.6 If additional facilities, such as storage tanks and booster pumps, are required to provide adequate service to an Extension and only that Extension, the cost of such facilities shall be charged to the Applicant. If such facilities benefit the existing system as a whole or are of a size larger than required to serve the Extension, the Utility shall absorb the cost of the facilities in excess of that required to serve the Applicant's development.

IV. ADVANCE-PAYMENT EXTENSION CONTRACT

4.1 An Applicant, on execution of an Advance-Payment Extension Contract, shall deposit with the Utility an amount equal to the Utility's estimated cost of the Extension. On demand, any additional amount that may result from increased costs as determined by the Utility shall be paid to the Utility, and the Utility reserves the right to delay installation of any Extension or service taps in any Extension until it has received such additional amount.

On completion, the Utility shall determine the actual cost of the Extension and shall refund the difference between the actual cost and the deposit, if the actual cost is less than the deposit. If the deposit is less than the actual cost, then an additional charge shall be made to the Applicant for the difference. Said additional charge shall be payable within 15 days of being invoiced. The Utility reserves the right to delay the installation of any service taps in such Extension until it has received the additional amount.

4.2 In the event that an Extension under an Advance-Payment Extension Contract is installed in a street or highway on which property other than that of the Applicant also abuts, the Utility agrees to require that such other property owners, before making any connection to said Extension for water service, shall pay an amount which, in the judgment of the Utility, is their proportionate share of the cost of the Extension. Such persons may pay such share on an immediate- or deferred-payment basis. Such amounts shall be refunded to the Applicant when received by the Utility. Total refunds on the contract shall in no event exceed the total amount paid by the Applicant. Copies of the original contract held by the Utility shall be properly endorsed by such new participant, giving effect to the cost-sharing provisions created by this section. The new participant will thereupon be subject to all of the terms, conditions, and provisions of the contract. A copy of the new contract will be furnished to the Applicant.

4.3 All liability for payment of refunds for proportionate sharing shall terminate 10 years from the date of the Advance-Payment Extension Contract, and any part of the amount paid by the Applicant not refunded within such 10-year period shall be the property of the Utility.

4.4 No interest shall be paid on the amount paid by the Applicant or any part thereof.

4.5 The Applicant and each subsequent participant in an Advance-Payment Extension Contract shall be entitled to receive a proportionate share of amounts received by the Utility from subsequent participants during the 10-year period referred to in Section 4.3, all as determined by the Utility, and shall be furnished with a copy of the contract endorsed by such subsequent participants.

4.6 The assignment by the Applicant or a subsequent participant of the Advance-Payment Extension Contract or any interest therein or of any money due or to become due by reason of the terms thereof, without the written consent of the Utility endorsed thereon or on an executed counterpart thereof, shall be void.

4.7 All Takers connected to Extensions installed in accordance with the terms of an Advance-Payment Extension Contract shall be subject to the applicable rates, rules, regulations, and terms and conditions of service of the Utility. However, when the municipality does not pay the fire-service charge for a particular Extension, said charges shall be paid on a pro rata basis by all Takers on such Extension in addition to their charges for water.

4.8 The Utility reserves the right to require that an Advance-Payment Extension Contract cover all Mains needed to supply a real estate development or subdivision in its entirety as provided in Section 2.6.

Rule for Water Utilities Making Refunds

4.9 For each residential customer with a ⅝-in. meter connecting to the Mains covered by the contract, the Utility will make a refund to the Applicant based on the revenues derived. Such refunds will be made during the period established by the contract. Refunds will be made only up to the amount of the original advance for construction.

V. DEFERRED-PAYMENT EXTENSION CONTRACT

5.1 An Applicant, on execution of a Deferred-Payment Extension Contract, shall deposit with the Utility an amount equal to 10 percent of the estimated cost of the Extension. On completion, the Utility shall determine the actual cost of the Extension, and the Applicant shall pay an additional 40 percent of such cost not later than one year from the date of such deposit and pay the remaining balance not later than two years from such date, together in each instance with interest on the unpaid balance at an annual rate of interest equal to the net effective rate of interest on the water revenue bonds of the Utility issued most recently prior to the date of the contract. If bonds have not been issued for the 12-month period immediately preceding such date, then the Utility reserves the right to set an annual rate of interest, as determined by the Utility, equal to that charged in the market place for municipal bonds. Interest shall accrue from the date the contract is executed by the Applicant.

5.2 An Applicant shall be eligible for a Deferred-Payment Extension Contract only if the Applicant furnishes to the Utility an irrevocable letter of credit of a bank qualified to do business in the state having a capital and surplus in excess of $20 000 000, which letter of credit runs in favor of the Utility and undertakes to make payment directly to the Utility in the event Applicant defaults in its obligations to make the payments called for pursuant to Section 5.1. The letter of credit shall be in the full amount of the estimated cost of the Extension without reduction for the 10-percent deposit, but shall not require payment of more than the unpaid balance of actual cost if less than estimated cost. In lieu of the aforementioned letter of credit, the Utility may accept a cash bond, bank passbook collateral, or other security acceptable to the Utility.

5.3 In the event the Applicant defaults in its obligation to make the first installment payment called for pursuant to Section 5.1 for a period exceeding 30 days after the due date, the Utility may accelerate any or all of the remaining balance due. Any installment outstanding 30 days after the due date shall be subject to interest at the same rate as unpaid taxes.

5.4 Applicant is responsible for attorney's fees and court costs incurred when the Applicant defaults in its obligations to make payments called for pursuant to Section 5.1.

5.5 If any installment payment and applicable interest is not paid in full within 30 days of the due date, water service to the premises may be terminated. This action will be taken whether or not the premises are occupied, and the Utility shall assume no responsibility for any resulting damage. A reconnection fee must be paid before the water service is restored, and any collections made at the premises prior to termination will be subject to a field-collection charge.

5.6 The cost sharing and other provisions described in Sections 4.2 through 4.8 shall also be applicable to Deferred-Payment Extension Contracts. The Applicant shall be entitled to receive a proportionate share of amounts received by the Utility from each subsequent participant during the 10-year period from the date of the Deferred-Payment Extension Contract, provided that any amounts to which such person becomes entitled and any advance payments made by such person shall first be credited to any balance and interest remaining unpaid under the Deferred-Payment Extension Contract or any deferred proportionate share payment.

Glossary

ad valorem tax A state or local tax based on the assessed value of real or personal property.

advance for construction Advance made by or on behalf of customers or others for the purpose of construction, which are to be refunded either wholly or in part. When an applicant is refunded the entire amount to which he/she is entitled according to the agreement or rule under which the advance was made, the balance, if any, remaining in this account shall be credited to contribution in aid of construction.

ancillary charge A separate charge for ancillary services that is not included in costs for general water service. Often in providing water service, the utility must perform these ancillary services, and these services often benefit only the individual customer using the services and have no system-wide benefit.

availability charge A limited-use charge made by a water utility to a property owner between the time in which water service is made available to the property and the time when the property connects to the utility's facilities and starts using the service.

capacity The ability of the water utility to have the resources available to meet the water-service needs of its customers. It is the combination of plant- and service-related activities required to provide the amount of service required by the customer. The plant facilities required are a composite of all types of facilities needed to provide service. It represents the ability of the water utility to meet the quantity, quality, peak loads, and other service needs of the various customers or classes of customers served by the utility.

connection charge The charge made by the utility to recover the cost of connecting the customer's service line to the utility's facilities. This charge is often considered as contribution of capital by the customer or other agency applying for service.

contract demand Relates to an agreement between the water utility and a large-use customer who requires a significant amount of the total capacity of the utility. The agreement would fix the terms and conditions under which the water utility would provide service to the customer. Such an agreement has been called contract capacity.

contribution in aid of construction Any amount of money, services, or property received by a water utility from any person or governmental agency that is provided at no cost to the utility. It represents an addition or transfer to the captial of the utility, and is utilized to offset the acquisition, improvement, or construction costs of the utility's property, facilities, or equipment used to provide utility services to the public. It includes amounts transferred from advances for construction representing any unrefunded balances of expired refund contracts or discounts resulting from termination of refund contracts. Contributions received from governmental agencies and others for relocation of water mains or other plant facilities are also included.

curb stop A shut-off valve attached to a water-service line from a water main to a customer's premises, which may be operated by a valve key to start or stop flow in the water-supply lines of a building. Also called a curb cock.

customer classification The homogeneous grouping of customers into classes. Typically, water utility customers may be classified as residential, commercial, and industrial for rate-making and other purposes. For specific utilities, there may be a breakdown of these general classes into more specific groups. For example, the industrial class may be subdivided into small industry, large industry, and special. Some water systems have individual customers (large users) with individual water-use characteristics, service requirements, or other reasons that set them apart from other general customer classes and who may require a separate class designation. This may include large hospitals, universities, military establishments, and other such categories.

dedicated capacity The portion of the water utility's total capacity that is set aside or "dedicated" for use by an individual large-use customer or group (class) of customers whose total use is a significant part of the utility's total-capacity requirement.

depreciation The loss in service value not restored by current maintenance as applied to depreciable utility-plant facilities. Depreciation is incurred in connection with the consumption or prospective retirement of utility-plant facilities in the course of providing service. This depreciation is the result of causes known to be in current operation and against which the utility is not protected by insurance. Among the causes are wear and tear, decay, action of the elements, inadequacy, obsolescence, changes in the art, changes in demand, and requirements of public authorities.

equivalent customer The means of relating large-use customers to a single family unit or other small-use customer unit, such as a ⅝-in. meter customer. It would represent a composite of all elements of cost differences between the unitary customer and the large-use customers to be served. Normally, it is expressed as a ratio of the small-use customer unit.

fire-protection charges Charges made to recover the cost of providing both public and private fire-protection service to the communities served by the utility.

future capacity The capacity for service somewhat in excess of immediate requirements that is built into a utility in anticipation of increased demands for service resulting from higher uses by existing customers or from growth in the service area.

government-owned water utility A water utility created by the state or other government-agency legislative action, with the mandate that the purposes of the utility are public purposes and that its functions are essential governmental proprietary functions. Its primary purpose is to provide its designated area with potable water in an adequate supply at reasonable costs so that people of the area may improve their health, safety, and welfare. A government-owned water utility may be part of a municipal government operation, a county agency, a regional authority, or take such other forms as is appropriate for its service area.

investor-owned water utility A utility owned by an individual, partnership, corporation, or other qualified entity with the equity provided by shareholders. Regulation may take the form of local or state jurisdiction.

monthly, bimonthly, quarterly user charges The charges made to the users of water service through the general water-rate structures of the utility for the utility's share of the cost of servicing the water-service requirements.

rate base The value of a water utility's property used in computing an authorized return under the applicable laws and/or regulatory policies of the agency setting rates for the utility.

service connection That portion of the service line from the utility's water main to and including the curb stop at or adjacent to the street line or the customer's property line. It includes other valves, fittings, etc., that the utility may require at or between the main and the curb stop, but does not include the curb box.

service line The pipe and all appurtenances that run between the utility's water main and the customer's place of use and includes fire lines.

system-development charge A contribution of capital towards recently completed or planned future backup plant facilities necessary to meet the service needs of new customers to which such fees apply. Two methods used to determine the amount of these charges are the buy-in method and incremental-cost pricing method. Various terms have been used to describe these charges in the industry, but regardless of the term used, these charges have the purpose of providing funds to be used to finance all or part of capital improvements necessary to serve new customers and are raised outside of capital to be served from general water-use rates.

system-development charge facilities Those facilities, or a portion of those facilities, that have been identified as being required for new customer growth. The cost of the facilities will be recovered in total or in part through a system-development charge.

unit cost The cost of producing a unit of a product or service. An example would be the cost of treating a thousand gallons potable water for use by the water utility's customers.

vintage rates A program in which customers are classified and customer rates are based on the date or period in which a customer connects to and first obtains service from the utility system. Such rates and charges can include user rates; customer contributions of capital for system development, main extension, connection fees; or for ancillary services rendered. The concept has been used during periods of rising average costs to reflect the higher costs associated with serving new customers.

Bibliography

The reference citations in this bibliography have been selected to compliment the topics discussed in this manual. A literature search of AWWA WATERNET's standard bibliography on *Rates and Costs of Service* will identify additional citations on water rate theory, practice, and related issues.

A Businesslike Approach to Fire-Protection Charges—Committee Report. *Jour. AWWA*, 66:1:22 (Jan. 1974).

BANKER, R.F. Tailoring Rate Structures to Wholesale and Large Industrial Customers. *Jour. AWWA*, 71:4:197 (Apr. 1979).

——— Allocation of Costs to Functional Cost Components. Proc. AWWA Water Rates Sem., Las Vegas, Nev. (June 1983).

——— & COSTANZA, F.B. Base-Extra Capacity Water Rate Design. *Jour. AWWA*, 75:9:444 (Sept. 1983).

BARDEN, D.S. & STEPP, R.J. Computing Water System Development Charges. *Jour. AWWA*, 76:9:42 (Sept. 1984).

BOLAND, J.J. The Requirement for Urban Water—A Disaggregate Analysis. Proc. AWWA Ann. Conf., San Francisco, Calif. (June 1979).

——— ET AL. Forecasting Short-Term Revenues for Water and Sewer Utilities. *Jour. AWWA*, 74:9:460 (Sept. 1982).

CLARK, S.C. & JUDSON, H.R. An Analysis of Delinquent Residential Water Account Shutoffs. *Jour. AWWA*, 67:5:264 (May 1975).

CORSSMIT, C.W. & GREEN, D.D. Water Utility Costs and Rate Design For Fire Protection Services. *Jour. AWWA*, 74:6:270 (June 1982).

COSTANZA, F.B. Considerations in Distributing Costs of Service to Customer Classes. Proc. AWWA Water Rates Sem., Las Vegas, Nev. (June 1983).

COTY, D.R. & GOODMAN, A.S. Cost of Providing Water for Protection. *Jour. AWWA*, 62:7:407 (July 1970).

Determination of Water Rate Schedules—Committee Report. *Jour. AWWA*, 46:3:187 (Mar. 1954).

FERRY, W.K. Connection Charges: One Way To Finance System Expansion. *Jour. AWWA*, 71:1:2 (Jan. 1979).

Financial & Operating Data 1983—Investor-Owned Water Utilities. Natl. Assoc. Water Companies, Washington, D.C. (1983). p. 37.

FONDA, S.H. Financing A Capital Improvement Program: Revenue Requirements, Cost of Service Analysis, and Rate Design. *Jour. AWWA*, 71:4:187 (Apr. 1979).

Fundamental Consideration in Rates and Rate Structures for Water and Sewerage Works. Joint Report. Amer. Soc. Civil Engrg. and Amer. Bar Assn. (1951).

GIFFORD, F.J. The Inch-Foot Method of Charging for Public Fire Protection Service. *Jour. NEWWA*, 46:12:370 (Dec. 1932).

GRIFFITH, F.P. JR. Revenue Systems—Some Design Concepts and Related Administration Considerations. Proc. AWWA Ann. Conf., Las Vegas, Nev. (June 1983).

Law and Water—Cities Not Prohibited From Charging Connection Fees. LaSalle National Bank v. City of Warrenville, Appellate Court of Illinois, Apr. 7, 1982. *Jour. AWWA*, 74:11:18 (Nov. 1982).

MATTHEWS, R.B. & WEBSTER, S. Cost-Based Water Rate Design. *Jour. AWWA*, 74:6:282 (June 1982).

METCALF, L.; KUICHLING, E.; & HAWLEY, W.C. Some Fundamental Considerations in the Determination of A Reasonable Return For Public Fire Hydrant Service. Proc. AWWA Ann. Conf., Rochester, N.Y. (June 1911).

MILLER, J.W. Old Water-New Water: Setting Equitable Water Rates For Suburban Customers. *Jour. AWWA*, 76:9:34 (Sept. 1984).

NOLAN, R.B. JR. & FORAN, R.E. Strategic Financial Planning. *Jour. AWWA*, 75:9:436 (Sept. 1983).

PITTS, H.W. Collection of Delinquent Accounts. WPCA/AWWA West Virginia Sec. Ann. Conf. Joint Meeting, Canaan Valley, W.V. (May 1983).

Private Fire Service Connections: Survey of Stand-by Charges and Meter Requirements. Engrg. Div. of Assoc. Factory Mutual Fire Insurance Companies, Norwood, Mass. (1959-60).

ROOT, D.A. & CAMP, T.R. Equitable Charges for Fire Protection. *Jour. NEWWA*, 69:3:90 (Mar. 1955).

ROULIER, M. Survey and Analysis of Bill Collection Procedures. *Jour. AWWA*, 68:9:479 (Sept. 1976).

RUSSELL, J.D. Seasonal and Time-of-Day Pricing. *Jour. AWWA*, 76:9:63 (Sept. 1984).

SALEBA, G.S. Financial Planning During Times of Economic Uncertainty. *Jour. AWWA*, 74:9:14 (Sept. 1982).

——— Revenue Requirements: What Considerations Are Important? Proc. AWWA Water Rates Sem., Las Vegas, Nev. (June 1983).

STROEH, J.D. The Real Cost of Water—Marin County, California. Proc. AWWA Ann. Conf., San Francisco, Calif. (June 1979).

Water Charges for Private Fire Protection. Natl. Fire Protec. Assn., Boston, Mass. (May 1961).

Water Rates. AWWA Manual M1, AWWA, Denver, Colo. (3rd ed., 1983).

Water Utility Accounting. AWWA, Denver, Colo. (2nd ed., 1980).

WOODCOCK, J.J. The Common Denominator: Equivalent Residential Units. *Jour. AWWA*, 76:9:56 (Sept. 1984).

WOODS, C.E. Principles of Discounting for Main Extensions. *Jour. AWWA*, 57:4:397 (Apr. 1965).

——— Similarities in Economic Theory and Sound Extension Policy. *Jour. AWWA*, 57:10:1289 (Oct. 1965).

——— Water Rates and the Rate-Setting Process. *Jour. AWWA*, 76:9:47 (Sept. 1984).

Index